TAMAZUNCHALE

*poetic and phonetic
irregularities*

Iván Argüelles

2021
LUNA BISONTE PRODS

TAMAZUNCHALE

© IVÁN ARGÜELLES 2021

*"Vayse meu corachón de mib,
¿ya Rab, si se me tornarád?"*
Jarchas

*Dedicated to the memory
of Mary Lou Willard*

Back cover photo by Raymond Holbert
Cover art & book design by C. Mehrl Bennett

ISBN 9781938521737
https://www.lulu.com/spotlight/lunabisonteprods

Luna Bisonte Prods
137 Leland Ave
Columbus OH 43214 USA

TAMAZUNCHALE

the nine hell-cycles
began when Cortés landed in Mexico
the nine hell-cycles
began when Cortés landed in Mexico

CONQUISTADOR BLUES

store the house of black pieces beneath
and just above hairline the diminished spaces
the attics of memory the recondite nooks
where stars go to die crushed by spatial envy
and tributes from temples and cuban cries
for deliverance as if angels in mock-black suits
wearing nooses and gilded ear-spirits what else
is audible within the chasm of yesterday's failed
lawn the epic of grass to darken in *the* montezuma's
fatal grasp the steps it takes to climb to the moon
a text with hands and paralysis of the left eye
who can play with this fetal verse will soon die
under wheels of pneumatic gravel the stellar stations
asunder in small blasts of methane the way an engine
moves through crowds of angry ghosts
plowing upcountry through vergers of snow-flowers
to dizzy splendors of brick and blood-shot wall
scattered crannies with Toltec microphones
hemisphere's siesta of artillery and feather
ancient seas moving through purplish air the dun
hills fetid with reminiscence of space travel
mournful valleys of shadow and loss the sound
reverberating of electric tires heading to eternal
south the consonant and drumming of the dead
twins and sons and fathers and all the grieving
of skies lamenting thunder in vacant houses moorings
of celestial fleets spiritually dead in search
of a water and floral displays in mirrors that
reflect nothing back and the acrimony of living
suited tightly in vestments of conquistadores
burning copal incense and worshipping phantoms
sierra after sierra of ineffable heights wasted
splendors lands ungovernable with jungle rot
pyramids inverted gaping at Mayan underworlds
far beyond the gypsy spangles of the dance
two by two the victims flayed heart-torn
wrapped in vinyl recording their tiny voices
for one last song and the conga lines going
round and round the big Hotel and to die
just like that in the midst of all that breathing
and neon boulevards and splash !

06-29-20

TAMAZUNCHALE

antes de abrir la demencia para descubrir
palabra tras palabra que no tiene sentido
¡ diccionario de pulmones ! ¡ pulgas y rascacielos !
para mejor comprender lo que pasa dentro del ladrillo rojo
al margen de la calle que nos lleva al sur donde
los muertos tratan de olvidar lo que pasó ayer
cuando la gran máquina de nubes y sonidos
se acostó al lado del mar que sufre tantas camas
inexplicables y sin eco y ahora dime ¡ qué quieres
con tus ojos apagados y tu mente como sirena
de ulises llamando a todos los náufragos
que la ambulancia está lista a partir !
ya me voy hacia la mejor tortillera que hay
para besarla en su coma de vidas paralelas
y entonces con una tristeza mundial
seguiré caminando un brazo mas famoso que el otro
una oreja de piedra y otra en ninguna parte
¿ para qué poner en dos el uno ?
¡ multiplicar significa morir !

07-21-20

HUĪTZILŌPŌCHTLI

it was the time they invented the lawnmower
a finger at a time and speaking an archaic Nahuatl
and the vestibular zones hazy with heart-muck
walls spattered with living gore , you know ,
temple artifacts and squatting chthonic goddesses
pissing on the map of Europe bull and all
the flayed hide spread out over the face
of the black Aztec sun come dawn on the
Sierra Madre del Oriente espy the flimsy
cardboard and tooth-pick fleet flying
the tattered silken banner of Castille and Leon
prelude to Buñuel's *los Olvidados* Jaibo
in tattered denim and the mangy black dog
of avenida Insurgentes and surrealism
in high alphabetic mode the grass flung in
all directions diacritics and spellbound a high
signal as if to make unhewn stone *talk*
a perennial human sacrifice for all ages
adolescent and senescent the virtues of hell
transmogrifications of newspaper routes and
hills pierced with inevitable longing for the four-fold
face of Brahma destruction and ritual
as depicted in the Pan-American codex of
the year 1953 climbing and ascending past
the divine possibilities of sky flattened

and the bottom encrusted with millions of dead
stars ! the evening of translucent violet spreading
its damp sheets over mountain peaks
snowy alliterations of the beginnings of time
mortal speech reduced to its basic three consonants
stuttered by hands and left deaf in the wake
when they picked up the telephone and
started the engines roaring all over again
and in her embroidery of eyelids and fox-fur
Malinche corn-dressed and picking out
of the furrows of a frozen wasteland the ghosts
spectra of plant and mineral life and
Lo ! the left-handed southern Hummingbird
ruby-throated glistening its eternal instant
and temples open with rot and stew
and motels flattered by the gods of insanity
we drove further and further south out
of a territory dominated by the State Hospital
and high school year-books and predictions
of ornaments worn like satellites of the moon
tomorrow will be different a Helter-Skelter
of disease and wipeout the clean slate
of the next universe come the demise
of the fifty two hells and their conquistador

07-23-20

THE STORMS OF MNEMOSYNE
"vestra est ista dies, favete, Musae"
Statius, Silvae, II.7, 20

Sisters of the hiatus and lacuna !
sing what ! grassy knolls verdant hills
childhood in a sequence of lapses
photographs faded beyond recall
who that was half-hidden in shrubbery
a stranger three times and hands
dedicated to harvesting distances
air and the foils of cloud and roof
situations lost to dreamy reverie
purple fillets ivy hymns and wine
gods strolling the midway disguised
as mendicants truants of love in rags
lore of the trodden stone the path
that leads half way to the stars and
goes dizzy spirals out of control
dust and the storms of Mnemosyne
raptures of bloom and seed yellowing
phosphorescent in the deluded eve
when night unfolds its stellar fringe
capturing one by one deluded mortals

a net of fireflies a sieve of bees stunned
by the lure of oblivion honey-colored
the raving moment of decease and
the world sent whirling underneath
where dear Proserpina in her pallor
counts backwards in her sleep
the months before the dawning
how few the lyric chords notes
ascending from spaces in between
vowels ringing with new silence
consonants discarded like leaves
before a sudden summer shower
was life this single moment was
the briefest catch of air and light
this your favored day O Muses !

07-25-20

THE DUBIOUS ANTICIPATION OF LIGHT

memory is not a feather-weight thing
balanced on the pharaonic scales but
all of space and gravity swelling in
the mind like a flayed Spanish bull
breath of blood and leaf distances
spanned by a single thumb the eye
can never reach hearing only vowels
in the vast eradicated paragraph of time
and such as we seem to be heading south
as always the destination of death
La Muerte ! the other who dwells within
clasps the ornate baroque syllable
that defies category and reason a physics
of cloud and atmosphere beyond our ken
lunacy and its adverse prophets standing
one rail above the hemisphere of doubt
twins in all but understanding *chaos*
and its fundamental missing echo a
version of indefinite articles disposed
by day's end in the cataract of thought
emanating from the small pool of sleep
darkening excrescence of ultraviolet
at the end of the tunnel the length
of ink and suppose we never really lived
suppose one of us was only a tattoo
on the shoulder of intellect and the other
but a filmy vapor suspended above an iota
subscript wavering between Greece and Turkey
the enormous Anatolian uphill of school
some two thousand years ago when Augustus
sat on his throne dreaming in French !

do we then just lapse into a photograph
in front of a motel on the Pan-American
a pair of squiggles in Mexican shirts
heading for the pyramids one last time
an hour of vagrancy and intoxication
music of serape and tapatio headache
that takes from our feet the poetry
of all recollection of that divine instant
when we couldn't have been more absent
from the totemic reality of inspiration
Hermano ¡ tú eres yo y yo no soy nadie !

07-26-20

THE ORIGIN OF POETRY
"surgite de vitreis spumosae Doridos antris"
                                    Statius, Silvae, III.2, 16

was poetry then the unspoken verse the glassy
mirage trembling in noon-time haze in some
anterior grotto of the mind a speculation of
matter and night not the soft-spoken but
the racing set of vowels the raging afterthought
the wrongly placed asterisks in the swelling
tides where sleep submerges the self in the warm
embrace of the Nereids prompt to drown the ego
echoing the vast differences between rock and air
subjective clause of delusion and spirit-hood
how did the second verse start and what was the
import of the caesura and hiatus and the loud
and maddened grief-cry of Thetis ? ask and ask
again the rolling hexameters and the dark cliffs
the wedged particle of sound purpled with divinity
and the oracle of salt and phosphorus enigmatic
as the fingerprint left on the leaf and of the voice
pursuing its own decibels in a fugue of melancholy
what can be uttered what must remain silenced
the approach of language in the serpentine when
dew and the distinctions of cloud and mist and
the unutterable aphasia of oblivion indecipherable
the spelling of words without meaning smoke
and the numbers lingering in the brain's half-lamp
does poetry then have no origins is it only a
syllabic entry in the catalog of unspoken desires
rotation of consonants in the mouths of seers
vacant-eyed and supernal in their punctuation
a sky floods with all that has been erased from
the archaic text stone fragments splintered bone
squiggles dissolving in an orient of sand and lotus
is it out of chaos that creation shapes its light ?
ooze and prattle of unreason the beautiful !

libation and duty of the mortal hand searching
as it does for the invisible script of memory

07-27-20

THE BUZZ AND HALLUCINATION OF THE MIND

they don't have the big Sanskrit texts I want nor the mountains
and their infernal silence and the way to trespass virtue
childhood spent on a dinghy going one way upstream
before the accident and the insurance clause the highway
the antecedents to the pronominal function fusion of
idiolect and reason fractions and quagmire the progress
of the foot and shoulder nor do they sell any more
the Socratic simples in the dollar store and the way
they look Oh when you finger the threads red and gold
that dangle from the crippled wire section of the counter
a loud a paraphrasis a fragment of sound the ultimate
aspect of glass under water and the fistful of antidote
the fiction of dialogue the two of us at odds with the hiatus
phases of the moon as written in old penitential hieroglyphic
battling with a surf of vowels for the upper hand
a televised retelling of the account of the flood or the Minoan
high sign for murder in the tenth degree gold-masked
Agamemnon you know the quarrel over the tub of fuchsias
and Cassandra carping about the ambulance and ride
back to the cemetery and the dog-faced deity of Lies
barking his marble accents pitch-black into the weave
of stars and intellect the way they're supposed to roll
out the cinema of light and here and there spackled
asterisks numinous entities of orthography schism and
diatribe the whole panoply of arguments for and against
breath and the principle of innocence the leaf and its
sadly coiled voice with instructions about where and
when to apply the cosmetic in Attic Greek circumflex and
dotted iotas all over the place nowhere to move jostling
in the crowd of dialects the uppermost Dravidian and
retroflex lotus and moonbeam describing the face or
faces of the *Woman-in-question* draped in her summary
of linen and gold fringed with assonance and distance
at last the ships sighted the fleet and barges of memory
burdened with out of control the dials and wasps the replete
with footnotes in cuneiform about approaches to the sun
the rising howl the dissonant blackening of its homophone
everlasting ! do we then do I assume you when the fix
in the arm the deliquescent time you sat by road-side
crying for the way that was lost and what was one to do
with the encyclopedia underarm wavering inconstancy ?

07-27-20

THE INVENTION OF MEMORY

the shape of the emerging leaf from its
green nothingness abide with *me* in dew
let the rays of the sun's mandala first
strike the portion of air called insight
a lark a distance unreachable by wings
bursts into song the ear enraptures if
sleep if the unconscious which both
precedes and supersedes eternity if
the hues imbued in the pool's surface
that narcotic darkness that inveigles
the eye awakening from its oblivion
who is the one to suffer the dissonance
in the grass running and with fast feet
the last to hold on and fall and who can
point a finger and say that was the one
when everything else all around breaks
into silence and skies looming from a
pre-birth of rock and glare the evidence
gathered in the palm of a small hand
sifting sand in the longing for shores
for the horizon that turns azure then
disappears in the changeless noon of time
a recording device in rock a vowel of
glass shifting in mid-air a branch a
tuft of weeds the little yellow flowers
called dandelions the voice that summons
them back to the dark stranger the whim
of wind and cloud to fraction thunder
at the onset of a July rainstorm and
who dives into the underneath pulling
at the skirts of unseen nymphs and
revives the next minute to tell of a thing
seen just once in the eerie emergency of
breath even as colors and sounds con-
spire to echo and vibrate in the numinous
recounting of chaos the inchoate origins
when finger fitted ring and ring circled
the unpronounced inch and all aflame
with brightness the mind began to count
sideways into the integer of lunacy
it is being alive and walking tracing steps
back and forth along the threshold that
separates mortality from immortality

07-28-20

CROSSING ROUGH SEAS LEAVING ITALY'S FIELDS FAR BEHIND

in my right hand was your birth
and in my left your unlikely death
the range and arc of what lay in between
embraced a lifetime in a few minutes
the awesome sky fractured by a lonely
vowel a pair of syllables perhaps
the race of running water no ear can hear
but cry for listening to the well dry up
stranger to the shape of air to the size
of wind come rushing down the dark
and seized by a monotony of light
you turned twirling like a detached leaf
in the full maelstrom of an unasked life
the divisions of breath and unconscious
mind the subtle field of a lost summer noon
how you lay motionless in the mirage
of memory nowhere to move nothing
to request the ancient sections of sound
that stored up in a single day became music
the lyre of Apollo the unstruck chords
ringing in the vestibule of the sea
such and such was the precious moment
wavering between what used to be and what
would never come to pass the hand with
its many fingers the grass darkening
underfoot the openings to the other side
replete with Minerva's winnowing fan
and the choir of stars abruptly concluded
whatever was meant to be foretold
the nothing of a whispered consonant
in my right hand was your birth
and in my left your unlikely death

07-29-20

***IT HAPPENED WHEN WE WERE
WALKING THROUGH THE PARK
THE SUDDEN SUMMER THUNDER
THAT TOOK ONE OF US AWAY***

which is the sum and which is the lack ?
does fortune once again retreat from clouds
and vitreous rains that scour memory
with a dozen invalid pasts the fierce and
troubling moment of indecision when
the motor wouldn't start and trembling
skies above subtracted their divisive widths
leaving us short-handed in the storm
a summer park a derelict labyrinth and
cries but coming from where and the reduced
fan of thoughts the bewildering weren't
you there too question mark and fused
to whatever the mind was grappling with
a consonant that begins with beta and
numinous versions of birthright and totem
as was expected death in her pinafore
of synapse and rust appeared unawares
at the curbstone hair in ribbons and half-
eaten lipstick her mouth awry with
threats who's next the adumbrating
vocalisms and in the rafters pigeons mourned
human intonations in the cooing and
you looking askance and doubting every
minute of your breath as the forward
motion of time propelled us both and sought
only to confound and reiterate its bleak
origins in some autumnal city by the cliff
what a fraction can do to eliminate even
the most complete integer and leaves
fallen by the way and our feet unsure
of which direction north was if sand
wasn't the best indicator a few more words
from sister death and the blotted sun of envy
we agreed to nothing but night-fall and
islands just glimpsed in the morning
now but sunken ruins dredged for gold
and LO ! was that Spain ? first and
mountain-shaped the looming threat
sleep contained and then loss the event
a chrysalis of red powders meant to
make invisible all recollection of
identity so weren't sure who of us
was which death had chosen that day

07-30-20

ANGIOLETTA IN SEMBIANZA

these days of anguish and tarnished splendor
lamps erased from the vault and secret tendrils
curling around senseless marble columns
what eye beholds if any the vestiges of beauty
raiment of celestial beings that used to sing
cloud and sun-bright dawns in archaic light
stone hoops rocky shapes of cliff and design
elemental vowels extended into the dark
a section of the hour dedicated to wings
seraphic gestures sustained by pure air
atmospheres that rush through highest thoughts
a mind a particularity of motion set into play
angelic semblance purity of memory in its
Latin template of meter and lost words
a sound of grass the longing for the other side
hills and woods of echo a dictation of greenery
the distance it takes a mirror to become
not just a reflection but its own loss
the grief which is life's summation an asterisk
meant to signal the ineffable instant
when love becomes so unbearable that all
else is a wasteland of unuttered syllables
a vision ! the emotion of leaves shaking
at day's end the oncoming density of night
Angioletta in sembianza shine just once more
in the midst of the constellations whose
shattered fortunes bear all of us away

07-31-20

GOING DOWN SOUTH TO SUNNYLAND

it's not as you thought a delayed hexameter
nor the routine of countless hours in glass
the fixity of forms between trees and what
they hold secret and the infinity of a cloudless sky
eventuality is only a motion unperceived
what lies beyond the mirror is death
we ask one another what the difference is
between noon and one o'clock if not the proximity
to a certain end and the elaborations of verse
are but remnants of a mind desperate to value
numbers the higher they get on the ladder
but the Pythagorean speakeasy of memory
is only a throne of ruins amidst phrases
that are outside the rules of grammar
longing and grief the sizeable cycles of omega
the famous eradications of myth and trumpet
and the yellowed sheets drawn over

the contours of a mortal identity
speak out ! tell me quick who is next ?
archaic viols unstrung harps flutes broken in half
the apollonian failure to reverse time
mountains of the western horizon !
dappled instances of hills yearning to echo
the small adumbrations of twilight
that ripple through leaves like the notes
imagined at dawn when the day's emptiness
commences little by little leaving no pity
for the souls condemned to repeat themselves
in the solemnities of writ and scope
to remember over and over the fierce
and ineffable romance of self-recognition
mother when was the last time we spoke ?
when we were going down south to *sunnyland*
and the deafened ear turned to stone
apogee of nocturnal constellations vibrato
and staccato at the dead-end of space
morse-code of fingers struggling to recall
a face lost in the grass one afternoon
the brief ritornello of light and breath

08-02-20

DEATH TO LAPO GIANNI AND HIS BALLADS

death to the champion on roller-skates !
death to the sidewalk that breaks his skull !
victory to all who have lapsed into coma !
a frigate bearing the rewards of breath has drowned !
death to the poem of retribution and sanctimony !
death to the all-around and losing gamblers !
so and so on and on and et cetera to unending verse
a section of polyphonic atmosphere is gone !
the promise of coming around again on the canvas
has been broken in two by a blade of grass
the ear lies there in the weeds unlistened
and hap of all turmoil the grief of hearing !
is it a wonder that in far off Sri Lanka the blues singer
has found the source of *his* turmoil and insomnia ?
death to Lapo Gianni and his ballads !
how often does the space-craft have to auto-incinerate
before we understand the message of true humility ?
death to the high-school home-coming queen !
death to the poet in his cups who tried to honor her !
Madonna and bliss and the fifty-six unities !
which is the shoe that will never fit and which
the route to eternity that requires no feet ?
the fiercest legend and most false the childhood
of innocence and infinite sleeping houses

the ambulances and x-rays and portfolios of aphasia
and junk and long afternoons in bad red wine
the essence of all matter is the iota of glass !
everyone on this side of the grammar lesson
lives in *italics* and lascivious centerfolds
and everyone on the other side of that lesson
dwells in the mountain of boundless ink !
nothing has been written that cannot be erased forever !
tantamount to tragedy is isolation from the vowel !
all hail the era of lies and mountebanks !
perpetual insanity and ritual devotion
brick and nail-file and black eye-liner
the queen is here ! hers are the eaves and the insects
the invertebrate heaven of solar homophones !
death to infinity ! death to infinity ! death to infinity !
small and round dots and whirligig asterisks
lunations that last several thousand years !
energy in the rock that idles on the road-side
the epitome of pre-history has not been uncovered
there is dust and flies with magnificent wings
iridescent and green and windows like eyes !
we are bidden to dream the organ-grinder's fist
lawns and rippling slopes and the sudden cliff !
death to the number One !

08-03-20

(for Jack Foley's 80th)
this twice was all
was meant to be this
thrice can never counted be
this eighty is a surfeit
a diamond claw a
twirling bachelorette a
governor in a swan dive
a virus dancing in a hive
cannot convince fourth
is aboriginal enough nor
why as slopes go the
eighty-first is swiftest
like an arrow meant to aim
the heart is nowhere to
be plumbed and orient and
fusilage burnt out unblessed
the rock n roll of time
blows thirty out of mind
the rest is last the last
is least the leaf still
lingering in the dusk

08-03-20

LOVE NEW AND ANCIENT VANITY

"Amor, nova ed antica vanitate,
tu fosti sempre e sè 'gnudo com'ombra:
dunqua vestir non puoi se non di guai."
                                        Lapo Gianni

love infant chthonic blind and naked
more like frail mortals than a god
in flight half-transparent hovering
like a death above sluggish summer waters
was nothing proven in defense of you
unholy littering air with senseless wastes
the heart's a convoy trapped in the defiles
mountains are less eternal than sky
air is no balsam for the dead of passion
lengthens each day you serve with grief
for why we plead with deities tattered
and in rags who prowl abandoned malls
when we ourselves are but shadows
denuded by our strange desires
did the hour's toll high on the hill
give us the right to complain of life's
brevity the shortened inch the desperate nail
the thumb and index of unflinching
wronged by our own betrayal of the light
each eye disproved by the dream it spelled
how distant still the compassioned drill
the steps forward and back in the dale
the longing for some fair *Angelica*
joust and turmoil with internal enemies
litany of ephemera the constant trial
and by day's twilight when fogged the brain
staggers to its tunneled bed to trance
and seas of infinite regret their tides raise
love's soft hand the drug offers to forget
but comes the dawn and arrows invisible that
pierce the mourning soul with remembrance
and down pure avenues of shade and green
does Venus spread her transient veil
anon and ever the deathly still and
books that turn to pallor and to ash
each vowel erased each intent denied
do then take flight from this drugged mind
and leave open pathways to Elysium
though we may never in there dwell

08-04-20

THAT LOFTY AND SUBTLE POETIC LESSON

those who have been taken from us
    I am tired of the reckoning
battle-field strewn with plastic toys and
where air once held sway dark avenues
    the trek to nowhere
a lesion of trees a section of cloud defiled
recalling recitations bright and sweet
on meadow mounds and murmuring groves
    the library of memory in the wind
shape of hand stain of grass and palaces
like ivory or glass shining in deep thought
    you became a shadow no longer quick
and underneath the turf the palpitating void
whose mansion ruined now stands still
with back-yard swings and boxes filled with sand
    small voices iterate the beyond
        echoing something never heard
grown to futility and age the mask of reminiscence
scattering radio waves with lyric tragedies
songs that alphabetize the ruin of our lives
    marmoreal once statues of sun and rain
we played between the ivy and the hill
running backwards through shapes of light
until breath stood still and eye turned blank
    envy of nymphs who run their fingers
    through summer's crystal rills
aloft espy the ephemeral dragon-fly whose hues
of pallor and regret take wing and disappear
exchange of form and memory we struggle to know
    a classroom of Latin verb and glassy waves
    the hero bound to his tethered ear
straining the fabulous music to hear and ropes
salt woven and strictures of scanned metric strophes
will never more come back the afternoon in braids
    loves and phosphates and calendars halved
by idling passion the dizzy engines of invisibility
and heavens with flute and ornate golden stitch
embroidering verses of enigmatic mortality
    taken from us repeatedly in dreams
and oceanic darkness the mind swells at night
with porches that flare with incandescent fireflies
the dance was meant to last the hour to never end
    it was poetry's subtle and lofty lesson
we strove to read even as we vanished from
one another in the bower of silent leaves

09-04-20

BLACK LIPSTICK

Andromeda liberata ! discovered at last
the lost music and frizz the retail lotion
that waxes the dawning of mind and the focus
and fission the least reaction to echo ricocheting
between mountain and myth the elaborate
over-stated regression into the archaic where *Puella*
labors over her Catullan sparrow's death the sadly
unconscious moment when parallel lives unwind
bifurcating into separate horizons one beyond
the other in a sunset of spiral and hexagon
what else is there but the solar homophone ?
great and wild the incredible retributions of hair
set up in combs and hives blackening in
the weird late afternoon heat and who wears it
and who struts on the Riviera Maya beach
in her loin cloth and amnesia but the *White*-Goddess
herself tender recall of lilac and ambrosia
histories of nail polish and eye-liner and finally
of *black lipstick* and the cinema of rejection
and platinum the quicksilver argent hypothesis
of death after life seen as a sequencing of moving
particles able to talk and revolve in sleep
and her arms upraised in devotional attitude
and her mouth opened to utter the great syllables
that none are meant to hear that bring nothing back
from outer space not even the missing echo of silence
her is Big ! *her* is a wonder ! *her* belongs to No one !
pidgin speech of mutilated statuary left behind
by the conquistadores and the slowly shifting matter
the quanta of vowels in disorder the alternate
reality which is the only real one et cetera
distances mount on distances small seas
come beckoning on their knees to wash the pebbles
her feet have trodden and whatever else
even as she vanishes pore by pore until only
her black lipstick glows in the deathless night
black lipstick is the holy thing
black lipstick is the unpronounceable
black lipstick is invitation to oblivion
what you and I can never own the *Goddess*

08-05-20

HIROSHIMA 75 YEARS HENCE

black sun that sets in the south this day
has forever spent its distance never more
to be seen but in ritual of memory and illusion
flagrant deceptions of grammar and rote
sibylline utterances flood the hagiographic ear
what rotundas of sky shattered by a single
marble finger the envelope of fogs ripped
open and scatter the restless drowsing deities
to directions hitherto unknown a mythic drone
that issues from the unseen hive of oblivion
overtakes mankind for whom reason has
lost all meaning and witless thoughts devour
themselves in the plenitude of ignorance
pagoda and temple steps adorned with haiku
and idiolects that stand for fragrances and pools
lotus and shrine of celestial beauties once holy
draped in chimera of earthly reds and now
blotted from mortal eye the revolving moons
of the eleven eternities established by fate's
immense clone to dwell ever and ever on
the bamboo mountain-top shining in purity
of form but for delusion of mushroom-cloud
rising from the orthographic trigger of the west
erase all sight of great cities of the plain and
shouting glee from metal wings and fabric
of lies oiled by ire and spite the fuming victories
of the charnel house and bedlam's isolation ward
do presidents not grieve even as they are sent
instantaneously to the thousand hells of stupidity
unfolding paper fans a million over that turn
to ashen residue the far corners of the universe
is today not the inverse of that holocaust
and earth's puny minions grovel in pestilence
forgetting before it has begun history's awful
but futile declaration of the end of time ?

08-06-20

DANTE VARIATION

ché la diritta via era smarrita
the stray way the lost the tangled
vines the mind entwined the fast
and stumbled rock and strait
ropes of saliva the hands bind
and eye riots in revulsion of
unseen dreams the way the straight
has gone away the fixed and
tormented obviated and skirmish
of words the plight of thought
the ancient egress through the fold
mountain and slope and twilight
blindness and not see more the way
strict and penitential the gravel
underfoot haunted by white
wraiths by what cannot appear
as sheets of light and moonlit
temple ruins and steps that shatter
the breathing mind the soul itself
on the way that is not found
the manner of dying the grasp
of lies the mummers who repent
along the way and tossed about
how can that be the way is lost
the foot unshod the route broken
by the simple print and inks now
dry and intellects that summoned
love now grazed and numbed
in bedlam's lonely cell

08-06-20

IN THE MAZE

"Dove se ne vanno le ricciute donzelle
che recano le colme anfore sulle spalle?"
  E. Montale, Ossi di seppia

the grand cloud formation to the left
of what the eye can see and the dense summer
weather a cycle of heat and menace
what the ear hears is residue of stone
or the lone bark of the stray shepherd dog
lost in a tumult of weed and briars
did we take the wrong turn when the
path came to an abrupt end inches
from the rubicund entrance to inferno ?
could still listen ear to the ground
to the remote howling the distance it takes
a spear to enter the Argive heart a pattern
that sets the pulse racing just thinking
about death the imminent even as sky
begins folding its sheets one by one at day's
finish calm lavenders and ocher hills
the loss and tedium of living through
still another day in exchange for what
in the barter between mortal and deity ?
where do the frizzle-haired girls go
who carry full pitchers on their shoulders ?
the enormous diffuse light over the grass
before dark sets in wrapping itself
around now senseless knees
from afar sound of wheels over gravel
need to lay the head down on rock
the temple with its dangling rusted gate
was never reached before sleep
heavy and immaterial took us

08-07-20

THE PRE-HISTORY *OF OBLIVION*

the buffer between the iota and the wound
when light was still green a pale absence
of the future and the sore in the mouth of the sea
by turns ruddy and cloudy waves came running
to the as yet ill-defined shoreline mist-draped
the strange and improbable line to the west a horizon
with puerperal fever and small ignitions
like the contention of shape and form and
to each and every was given the lip of understanding
and a second lip to forget that understanding
if a mouth was formed and the need for love
and the hair-line excised from the mask
and before pottery was glazed and a loud rising
from the tide bringing to the dream a surface
of neglect and toil to wake to that on the other
side of ferment and desire who could efface
that section of sleep and sighting high
in the myriad night a sky trembling with asterisks
emotions and punctuation of grass and clay
given to the word a separate vowel and perforce
the material from which syllables gain strength
oracular and devastating when put to the test
hives and trees and the first bird to dawn
with song and charity should the need arise
when music comes from the street without sound
the effect of children becoming antler and hoof
in the bestiary of the heavens innocence in hues
of twilight and the suddenness of bats swooping
to take from the ardent mind a folio of
ineffable thoughts with which to combat the Wheel
days and days before time the small and sad
outposts where ambulances take voided souls
in search of bodies of caves of glistening promises
tomorrow is an abstract version of matter a solemn
divagation between roads that do not exist
what is yearning but the consonant without echo
how can so much darkness issue from a single leaf ?

08-08-20

BIRTHDAY ODE FOR JACK FOLEY

"le inutile macerie del tuo abisso"

                                              Montale

deaths *the* death weights the shoulder bears
ragged and tortured hemline of the sun
this astral burning we call summer
how many are left for you to count ?
can you still hear the air breathing ?
culmination of eight decades this day
is it for you to celebrate or to grieve ?
as the ninth decade the least sure starts
an infirm and tottering walk into obscurity
you wake today rising from a bed of sorts
in your head poetry's waxen verses play
a round of pale anthologies and fields
so far off they lack all ten horizons
a flood of light and shadows leaf and rock
trimmed edges that no longer feel
the ancient pilgrim's cry when he has
at last espied the mirage of his Jerusalem
chorus of tinsel jazz and cymbals
notes of the archaic Delphic flute
the Lamp ! turns to stone the ear's
sweet unwinding dream of sound and song
fire-flies and crickets in hidden glass
more remote than ever and insane
the movie flickering in the brain
perhaps you can tell yourself that now
only now you are just beginning to *know*
all else is the flim-flam lyric of a man
adrift on a paper boat a tattered sail
and winds that rush from nowhere
to bear him into the endless dark

09-08-20

AND A BIRTHDAY ODE FOR MARILLA

golden diphthongs and silence !
the longest blade of grass is at the door
and choirs of seraphic cloud and rains
that last forever and a day though sun and
oils and the thousand vagrant rays of light
that peer through cracked walls and vines
the hills of an unsighted west and memory
of the barge floating downstream that
bore you through the quandary of birth
into the lamplit zone where the dead
dear to your heart flit in angelic trance
how can you bear this solemn gravid day
but with the joy of unspent vowels and loud
the untethered sky with which you dream
another life lies straight ahead with its
mountain of marvels and heights only knees
can reach the gilded flute of time its
first and last notes waking in your ear
and in your breast the recollections
of the day on earth you survived and grieved
only to move on to this summit of years
and small catastrophes the sewn embroidery
of thoughts your mind spills forth with glee
you are at last the one you meant to be
golden diphthongs and silence !

08-09-20

ALTERTUMSWISSENSCHAFT

                      these greco-italian people
how could I ever have abandoned them ?
rock salt and squid corpses drying in the sun
Picasso could not have painted squint-eyed
this scene of women drifting by in languid skirts
sea-colored thread-bare their long legs
thighs burnished by the sun of late antiquity
temple ruin in the left eye bandage of Persian wars
resolving the right eye and the ear a flood
of laminated echoes drained through lava
and in the shape of lunar transgressions
a heat in folded circles and diaphragms and
drugs to make the heart stand still
while the easy sky of Tuscany transports
a grief of the millennium through thick coats
of acrylic and Penthesilea and long afternoons
wheeling the strings of faintly dyed ocher
hill-slope tan the dun and din of the agora
or the roman forum under its torn umbrella
the roar of gladiators and spears the size of time
pierce the lion's keen sight and verses mixed
with thyme and basilisk the great roving hexameter
that brings Trojan exiles back to their stony fates
does Carthage's queen still smolder or Cleopatra
clasp to her breast the asp ? alphabets come and go
a script of submarine intelligence porphyry
and eglantine the bards declaim strutting
in their bath and suicides of emperors and small
teeth that cling to flowers in the dust
does time finally make its exodus among these
abandoned souls ? do we mark our history books
with hyacinth and lavender purring in depths
of a grammatical sleep and vowels ascend in hues
the oracular voice a drowsy wine-dark drone
that inveigles the dying breed of man
into consonants of endless night
basalt noon of a blackened sun ?

08-09-20

IL POMERIGGIO

no more bound to earth than to heaven
the weary year more than half its calendar spent
straddles the signal to cease while plunging
forth into an air of riddles a non-existent future
today a spare lawn spreads out toward the west
silence and music of extinguished candles
the eye's margin contracts ever more before
the vanished or decayed beauties of —
the ancient temple of *love* ruins of thought
and asterisks a smattering of dots flicker-
weaving where the hill places its foot and
the brow of the cliff and the menacing weather
predicted by the Sirens when will it occur
who will be the last to become a cipher and
the immense cavity out of which insects
with the names of old girl-friends issues
a foray into the erosion of marble and books as
if this were the hour the mid-point the noon
and still the days rush out of control with their
winds and epicycles and impediments to movement
nocturnal skies already visible three in the afternoon
planets and the punctuation of dead suns
heaving like dust motes into the quarry where
ghosts of mules and carts tarry sluggishly
back and forth over the great hoof-print
of the oracle and what is that singing that
devastates the ear with an extravaganza of 1589 ?
such is the day's catastrophe that mortals
are forbidden to meet and squabble smoking
and the desire for one more gin and tonic
a cascade of syllables announces the penultimate
day on earth ! gone are the arcadian measures
of literature and science prominent with vowels
of grace and leaf and the enormous episode
erroneous and turbulent of progress has come
crashing into the plate glass window of politics
a museum of tombstones stands on the edge
beside the refuse and recycling heap and warnings
elicited from the spirit-reader in her blind of canvas
and bitumen are no longer heeded –
hush and monotone the music of the street
that no one can hear // postponed
none can gather // long and dreary afternoon
when the polygamous gods dawdle watching
motel earth burn in the bluish haze

will the past convey its trembling wooden horse
night-times into the walls of the secret city ?

08-10-20

THE WANDERING TOMBS OF TIME

the ban the scutcheon the arrows
sentient and larval beings white-eyed
dun the imitation Christ listing in the harbor
do big boats bearing Ulysses and crew
then sink slowly into the margins and
the voice of the waif and the brigantine
weaving the flogged sailor of admission
and the threads of crimson Parcae
the holy sisters of Dread you know them
crippled of knee and faint at close of day
their once nimble fingers prodigies of grass
the ultimate peninsula of benzene and spit
which are symbols of yearning as the universe
splits in two at the helm and the midnight
dross the fictions of plenitude and gravity
like the promises of reincarnation and light
what eye can bear the silent crashing bolt
thunder-streaked anterior sky of Zeus
the beast at the throttle the multiple hand
the mythographer blind to his sutures and what !
ankle deep in consciousness the envoy
of the Underworld Thoth or Hermes with
globes of pure crystal in either fist and loud
the roaring adjectives of merit and judgment
who will place the small corpse on the Wheel
and anoint the passing star aiming for its
correlations and the heights and the furious
width of the inch between the waters that
punctuate the separate hemispheres of memory
the very statue of summer tall and remote
headless and swimming of unformed thought
a cry from its depths a profound verdure
the inkling of life to be and the sudden and
rapier like thrust of darkness to all come
as unawares as the echo of an unknown vowel
hidden in the mists and tartans of time
unfolding wired and woven into the inky
vast of night the inevitable and Lo !
do we learn to speak only to grieve ?

08-11-20

THE OBSCURE REGION WHERE YOU DESCENDED

does water have a divide between depth and surface
or is the illusion of a sun reflected in either dimension
the mainstay of why we keep our distance ?
the dead on a whim revolve imperceptibly in the air
that winnows itself inches above the impenetrable
breath without body the silence of their accents
and the density of their consonants left hanging
in the clarity of high noon and yet our ears catch nothing
of the phrase and etymology of their memories pallid
washed away in the first moments after the negative
has been developed and the flesh captured by the light
appears as nothing more than a spiritual misgiving
there is no reincarnation no double of time or space
no alternate to the flight of thoughts from their source
the number three may be all there is a cipher to puzzle over
the enigma of being born the essentially irreversible
minute by minute we live in hesitation of the end
doubt with its arcadias of love and anguish the serpent
that enters the self when least corporeal and lying
in grasses of a summer purloined from the eternities
of the Wheel ! and whom do the gods undress today ?
what's to celebrate because another year has ceased
its count and the glass that separates within from without
is simply not there no matter how much you hear ivy
scraping against the illusory wall the verbatim existence
of leaves and the dense foliage that erupts at night
dreaming there are larva and incorruptible vowels
somewhere deep inside the persons of the mind –
does daylight break its oath ? see the unruly sun
blackening on its inevitable course towards mountains
and the deeper seas of endlessness and watch how
each fob of the stop-watch snips off its bit of infinity
you have descended now forever into the depths
guided by no Virgil into the obscure regions where
memory unravels and the distant pounding of waves
against a surge of rocks and the opaque germ
of existence fades in the stellar conjecture of time

08-12-20

**IN THE CORNFIELDS OF ETERNITY
JUST BEFORE THE END OF TIME**

the unknown shape of the leaf
in the month named after the
first Emperor & heat turning red
texts of soil and grasshoppers
love ! before death had a hand
in it freezing the sky into immobility

leveling even the gods who claudicate
in their empty marble drawing rooms
was it an end to everything when
we kissed wildly in the open air
sweat pearling the mind and drone
of motorized insects the ear a future
of withering yellow grass eyes the color
of hay and the illegibility of corn
growing in the midst of verb conjugations
without person number and tense
chalk fingers the infernal blaze of
mouth wedded to mouth dank endlessly
swooning darkness the chthonic
present an inch of mulch residue
how distant the legends of Earth !
savage loam white roots wriggling
blind worms in their infinite galleries
plowing Pluto's ashen garden
mysteries of the adolescent Heart !
the secret lake of abandonment
purity of excess and skin-dazzle
ornament of a thousand black suns
setting in the pupil of the eye as it
goes blank with lunatic oblivion
a hand that measures nothing at all
another hand that becomes cloud
and the prediction of lightning
metal against metal the friction
that ignites and pulverizes fields
fragments of grain and mill-stone
how many motel rooms can Zeus
occupy simultaneously ? eighty-one !
does one ever get home again after
a night in the maze of falling stars ?
together with shoes untied blouse-
buttons undone the quicksilver
that zigzags through the brain
one last time before opting to die
full of the crimson bed of asterisks
brilliant punctuation of the eyelid
like a death warrant in triplicate
would one steal sulfur and chrome
just to get behind the mythic skies ?
darkening route of nostalgia unlit
remnants of the day's betrayal
listening for an underground stream
to bed with leaves of unknown shape
sweet indulgence followed by grief
the drum that is stilled in the wrist

08-13-20

THE IMMOBILIZED SKY

with so few days remaining jettison
the history books volumes of thorn and anticipation
learned nothing from their graphs and lies
rock strewn fragments and illusory lamps
the detritus of a single summer spent in the drug
details of memory like screw-pine and grist
the needles that never pointed north while
sailing with Ulysses into the bankrupt isle
how did we come this far being so unknown
and unknowing algae and tree-stumps
landscape dazed with uneven portions of smoke
the pit and the door the ice-box and the front-
lawn placed side by side and ivory and fennel
youth goes by like that ! a sudden squall in July
rain coming down in torrents sheets of lye
the planets honing their remote lenses
come into view for a fraction of a second
are you listening ? how much time is an hour ?
to kill a god deny him the honorific pronoun !
what is left to us already spent choirs of dark
section after section of dew the hemline
of the future dissolved in a drop and the dead
who come back with broken cups a deceit
to have worshipped their ashes – it is we
that are dead moving furtively from sleep
to sleep the agonies of still another trial
called daybreak and the petty thefts
that inure us to the greater absences of love
and the adamantine matter that wavers between
diagnostic and reduction what is it Plato said ?
to what unopened page do we owe our daily fate ?
filling bags with useless words with litanies
threnodies plenitudes of lunacy the stamp
and woof of the five o'clock carillon like thunder
ringing brass the heavy tongue of oracles
brazen syllables the beast at the wheel wearing
ornaments borrowed from fashion models
stiletto-heel shoes dense black eye make-up
dripping with a desire to ken the distances
that separate the various universes from
the One universe of *time* and what does it matter
each grammar rule each suspended vowel each
practice session of the false Spanish of the orient
and whittled down to the final minutes when mind
has no recourse but to turn to quick-silver and
the alloys of forged memories smolder in their
task of oblivion and betrayal what's to say and
what's to do and where to flee when the burden
a single blade of grass weighs on the scales
of justice and yes the days of youth burn
like tinder in the eye and the jargon
that kept us believing in the other life on high

only knee and shoulder wrenched from their socket
and the caryatids and ephebes we used to woo
but smatterings of shattered stone or marble chips
the reckless delivery into the crematoria
of all the shapes and sizes we yearned to be
más allá de la vida

08-13-20

THE LAST OMEGA
*"Not I – I alone fit no masks
    but cast joy and sorrow behind me"
       Odysseus Elytis*

hinges fobs and trinkets of the secret poem
punctuation that exceeds the thought process
renewal of what ? darkest sleep the dense
why wake three in the morning in the mind's
empty airport ? decision to eliminate words
excise syllables pronounce dead vowels long
misplaced corrupted by grammar violated by
history marching backwards as it were with
shadows the error and pomp of memory fix
and tool of the weary head and looking for stone
a rock anything solid to place it down to rest
running over with invisible finger tips the Greek
characters the absence of pity as Achilles you
know gets it and heads straight down into a
post-card Hades and listen to ruminations in
the void of archaic masks now and then forgetting
their lines missing the cues become suddenly aged
in the whisk of a minute outside and the threat
of rains forty days long and the heights never
to make it there and the ear has its islands just
as the eye its cycles of heat and foreboding of
planets off course ellipses and theory of space
duplicating itself but is it for humans mere pro-
jections of idea and mirage to ponder the ends ?
I am Orestes ! the victim of myth and denial
the *FURIES* hunt me down quarry of poetic miasma
no longer fleet of foot unable to take three steps
on the stairwell at a time plunging instead into
the vacuum where my ghosts wait to embrace me
and I promise to cease this verbiage this ineluctable
struggle with the lexicon preposterous strings of
consonants on a rosary of dust mounds ant-heaps
would-be mountains in an illusory west inhabited
by the Hesperides whose fading dance on the pulpit
of eternity is a last gasp of picture-book childhood
a system of belief in the *other*

and so there it is the precipice and mourning
what small creatures we be waking and dim and
opening the blinds to let shine for a brief whatever
the blackening sun and I am without luster a
token an isolation a forager of recollections
a music without notation a running out of

08-14-20

(UNTITLED POEM)

surely not of me you direct this paean
to a man of secret and a fool of sorrows
esteemed by none the mountain hides his heart
shadow bears him by noon shadow disappears
even as light breaks its spine upon the cone
he turns to face those other days
summers that reddened in an instant
the flash and bright of joy ephemeral
a constant vanishing into a void of matter
night him seeks to drown amidst a panoply
of fireflies asterisks and fading gods
how many moons to strike in a single dream
by his grass bound finger by his integer
of leaf and memory the hidden vowel
REPUBLICAN CONVENTION 2020
the gold ear-rings of rhetoric are invisible !
storm the podium with a brace of rabid pups
with shirt and tie and fields of buried memory
what mountebanks these human beings
strutting and prattling on a paper stage
armor and vessels of republic and democracies
the world's a tin can a powder fuse a junk heap
tuned inside out its eyelids burning so none
can see what ignorance lies within
case after case of broken promises a deficit
of morals and ethical bankruptcy a pride
to renown and issues of property and guns
void the cash and pockets filled with IOU's
how many words for gold can stand the test of time ?
dry bamboo forest clinging to illusory mountain side
in a flicker the wild fire and its myriad lapping tongues
lays to waste the thousand cities of Moloch
and Babylon and Jerusalem sail with broken
wings into the Jihad of endless bickering
boundaries of seas and irrigation ditches
wet backs and the ghosts of buffalo linger
by the place where the parasite and louse claim
strategic victory over mortality did not
disease and prejudice eradicate their whims
tossing into the sulfur pitch parasols

and bowling balls with purloined strikes and
bluffed puttering across Manitou's stolen lawns
representative government is the colossal lie
the selfish virtue the befogged shop window
the illusory tent where idiots hawk their wares
money ! confused sequence of consonant and cipher
the pink and poisoned crab-grass of stocks and bonds
prices rise people starve bread is exploded
on the sinking wharf of manifest destiny
look to the south where Montezuma sits in chains
look to the far west where the I Ching scatters fates
burning as vedantic bonzes before the universities
burning ever more as the microphones amp up
the galore of stridency and pettiness
encyclopedias that lack alphabets and ant-heaps
where in the dead of night politicians crawl
hoarding remnants of gunpowder and credit cards
shadowy symbols spectral vomit nightmare
the shape of distance is but a corpse
the torn leaf the soundless voice
echo of a history they never knew

08-26-20

THE SECOND DEATH OF MARY LOU WILLARD

how often does the music go silent
and where has the extra body gone ?

fear of death in the uncontained vowel
gone into the pale fast growing blank

vocative ascension heights of ocher cliff
Spanish lessons in retrograde sunlight

granite is the audible hemisphere of statues
whose heads are still waiting for the chisel

either this life or the next doesn't matter
can never have back the *first* number one

there was a moment of absence then motion
resumed its dereliction of circularity

conjugated the corn in separate summers
heat the dissension of ciphers becoming loud

went to the west side of town and Lo the Mall
with its brand-new cellophane prepositions

how little space crammed into the doorway
senseless gabbling of a hundred morning students

a life away from the origins and mouths
still red from passion's secret raging

it is not love at first sight but a thousand eons
of rock fragment evolving into small black suns

I promise to never if you promise to always
vows made to the grass of a court order

the stone mason is still working on the sky
while his daughters dress up for the prom

a button-hole filled with white ampersands
a night that has no evacuation plan

in the back seat of an automobile driving
into the bitter Lake of unwritten thoughts

language useless sounds put to the Wheel
disoriented mind that separates from matter

when a snow-flake gets tangled in the eye
then does the world vanish in dark asterisks

hard to believe time is just an insect waiting
for its translucent wings to grow and fly

in the other world summer was a cryptic noon
eyelid of an engraving hidden in a false July

we sat for days in the movie theater's afternoon
when night arrived we had become deaf cataracts

suddenly darkness prospects for a new planet
shining and not shining the lost syllables of Mu

all the words we ever could have exchanged but
muffled fractions of echo in the reverie of silence

holding on to each other in the frozen alley
metal came into being and the impenetrable

underneath it all the forbidden skin fragrant
with the faint perfumes of distance and rumor

a touch a leaf a stem twined around a petal
no color but the hue of broken glass in winter

can four years be nothing more than the eclipse
of sun and moon and the thirty ancient gods ?

collapse and excavation of the Masonic temple
telephones nymphs caryatids and death

angels have no backsides and cherubim lack skin
celestial moments only begin in oblivion

cannot articulate whatever went before
sun's terrible homonym moon's drugged eye

have lost it all have ceased to recall that
memories originate in swimming pools

shouts are red cries of awful glee ears stopped
in the vast hiatus that occurs at time's demise

ravaged cormorants that have gone astray
beryl and onyx eviscerate day's bright oracle

Mary Lou you were the current form of *what*
passing through the blushing gasoline of passion

Mary Lou today is nowhere on the stellar map
a dot a friction an errant whiz the circumflex

Mary Lou you fault punctuation for being strict
it's all noise a moment none can apprehend

driving your brand new car through sea-grottos
pressing your hands into cyclical shapes of ether

Mary Lou you became a six-year disease
a fear that overtook the highway to the North

someone put a hole in your fence someone wired
the rooms where your phantom yearned for more

what was it you never wanted to know
what was the keen enigma that tore your heart ?

Mary Lou two is more than just a way of being
it's the preterit junction of space and eternity

new mown grass hay and wild August skies
clouds that evaporate inside your palms AOI

you read the text that contains your name
you tossed the bones and said goodbye

09-08-20

DESDE MI NIÑEZ EN TENOCHTITLAN

la historia no tiene hemisferios
ni rodillas ni arena en sus ojos
la historia no tiene dos mitades
ni tampoco orígenes ni fin en
su larga recapitulación de mentiras
y promesas y por cada lado del río
donde yace semi-muerta la historia
hay al menos tres cabezas por cada
palabra desconocida que flota
todavía sobre la piel azteca que
cuelga desde la soga invisible
de los pirámides del sol y de la luna
y si uno va con pies de cucaracha
borracha por toda la carretera
Panamericana bailando y cantando
esas canciones estúpidas de la
radio *gringo* hacia donde va a acabar
en que sierra maestra espectral
de un sur que es nada más que
un cementerio enorme de dudas
que emana el sol negro de la muerte
calaveras de azúcar huesos hambrientos
dedos de yerba buena y caras
de ropa vieja sucia de cien años
sin lavar cuantas veces tenemos
que llamar a ustedes desde sus
desfiladeros de heridas y sangre seca
para regresar hacia el mundo de
la luz donde viven los abuelos
de piedra y llanto donde secan
su pelo eternamente mojado
las ninfas con nombres como
Rosario o Carmen todavía puras
como el día de su nacimiento
en el polvo de las estrellas giratorias
de la pre-historia esa era de árbol
y nube y pronombres sin identidad
No! la historia no tiene razón ni mente
y hay días que sufren hombros de humo
y semanas enteras de nostalgia
por techos donde caminan los fantasmas
de Chabela y Guadalupe !

09-10-20

LA VEJEZ DE MI JUVENTUD

si sigo adelante
              no sé donde ir
todo va para trás
no más los relojes saben volar
¡ tinieblas color de vino a mediodía !
¿ como puedo entender lo que dice la hoja
en su hora de tres mitades ?
ya voy por los senderos que nunca
han existido y todavía el sanscrito
de mi mente se clava a pájaros invisibles
tú dirás que soy mortal por dos minutos
que no tengo brazos ni alas sino pedazos
de sufrimiento en forma de palomas
la verdad es que ni sombra soy
ni memoria de veranos de agua
alguien que camina con rodillas pesadas
y los sesos ahumados sin dormir
si pongo en mi bolsillo derecho
todo lo que me enseñó mi madre
¿ qué pondría en el bolsillo izquierdo
sino acequias y nubes de tabaco ?
hasta mañana tendré que ir
siguiendo unos huesos comilones
que hablan toda la noche en peruano
¡ y a despertar en una montaña sin peso
en un mundo sin ayer !
hay horizontes de heridas humanas
donde nadan en sueños de piedra
los únicos hijos del dios de la escalera
y hay cielos donde caben alfabetos
y lenguas de tenedor y cuchara
en busca de su cuchillo eterno
para cortar lo que no tiene cuerpo
¿ porqué me gasta el olvido ?
no sabe nada la persona que habita
mi identidad de tantos años pueriles
¡ y yo que sigo pataleando al sur
porque no puedo ir al centro !
y todavía me voy listo a ahogarme
mientras mi abuelo va escribiendo
un nombre que no recuerdo

09-11-20

NACER SIN NACER

tengo un pronombre que no sabe caminar
y dos ojos al lado derecho que repiten la palabra *codo*
y me voy preguntando a cada estatua que encuentro
¿ para qué tengo que morir ?
mis rodillas tienen almas de puro sufrimiento
mis recuerdos no tienen nada del pasado
no más memorias del olvido en paises subcutáneos
catedral de mármol y benzina a dónde vas ?
en cada esquina hay hombres que escupen la palabra *pinche*
porque no saben que el oriente ya va ahogado
¡ y si hablo con ellos cuchicheando en sus orejas
unos *carajos* de piedra gastada desaparecerán !
no me encuentro hoy en ninguna parte
escucho pero no hay viento no más vocales rojos
¡ incendios de la purísima santa en su ataúd de fieltro
mírame ! con una mano afásica y la otra con su norte
¿ como puedo desengañar a la gente ?
ya han pasado las mitades de unos números desconocidos
y todavía está pasando el infinito del colibrí invisible
todo lo humano que no es mucho está en el hombro izquierdo
con sus corazoncitos naranjos y una debilidad para dolores
del subconsciente ¡ qué felicidad ! ¡ me caigo sin caerme !
la última vez me nací fumando en una escalera al este del tiempo
la próxima vez fumaré otra vida sin nacimiento ni dirección
¿ qué chistes son estos hermano ? vivimos al sur
donde el tiempo no existe y las olas de un mar ciego
corren para atraparnos en sueños de arena triste
pero la parte que no entiendo y eso es mucho
está escrito en un japonés del mediodía cuneiforme
¿ para qué tengo que morir ?
y dicen que si seguimos caminando sin sombras
llegaremos un día a los pirámides de Teotihuacán
tú con tu sol de estrábismo negro y yo con mi luna de amfetaminas
primero perdí a una muchacha de paladar albigense
luego a una de aljófar cubano ¡ pero las dos sin alas !
hay que escoger entre el terciopelo y la seda
entonces crecerá sin saberlo la hierba hilvanada de la muerte
¡ y no me digas que hay un lugar bajo la vereda en frente
que se llama *Infierno* ! hay ángeles sin huesos
que vuelan entre las paredes nunca vistas del cielo
y ciudades enojadas tambien que nadan sobre ilusiones
como si lo único que hacer fuera abrazar un diccionario
donde caben todos los sonidos efímeros ¡ pero
ninguna palabra entera ! ¡ yo soy una nube y nada más !
niebla de mis abuelos fosforescentes y pies tan lejanos
que hacen llorar a los zapatos desalmados de la vida
¿ para qué tengo que morir ?

9-12-20

AFTER A LONG ABSENCE

born after decades of flight and anxiety
me the self the puny otherness of distance
come calm the tumult of this irregular pronoun
evict from mind its satellite projections
of fame and toothless glory the fuming
and acid down-spell the hastened path toward
the you know how to write it marmoreal
on its stone of genuflection and longing
smaller voices the tiny decibels of a vowel
omitted from the panoply of sounds once
rounding the spires of air the ineffable
columns of memory the insatiable if you
will but reject this paper and erase the un-
founded thoughts about and the riverrun
of its method the peak of absence I mean
just reading the liner notes and calculating
the parallel ages of either the body or its
shadow whichever reaches the finish line
last or the first to recall oblivion and alpha
the fist of numinous errors the script and
its conjecture OK so it's a mistake a fuse
ready to blow an organic emblem lunatic
and assuring you can't have it both ways
et cetera me the irrelevant derelict phoneme
on the left-branching grammar of stolen
love the inching towards eternal grief
the consonant dislodged from its sound
I am less than that a white-out on a page
torn from the ream yeah the brief but
infinite dot shifting across an equinox to
disappear forever from the Bible of time

09-13-20

RED-FLAG WARNING

among the thousands of Mondays why *this* Monday ?
fearful and apocalyptic eye in which the universe pivots
more off beam than yesterday and in the coarse Latin
of the volcanic tavern the niggling customers drunk
in their afternoon swath of envy and ire perspiration
folded under a few mental creases and Hurrah !
for the sports squad of choice maiming the elephant
will it ever be perceived as better this awful riot
the out-of-control civil guard and uniformed muggers
who hold each corner in check lest whatever they
think might happen the whole thing swaying back
and forth against the goal-posts you know the story
the casual forays of Nemesis into the untold minions

the skies with their petrol angels ablaze and wingless
deities in Brownian movement between cloud-bursts
is it a wonder the x-ray machine has ceased functioning
that parking lots fill with ash from a distance twenty
thousand miles away where mountains ignite themselves
out of despair the forest primeval gone in a trice erased
from mortal memory and what the hell each minute of
each hour is the fatal ticking away plundered sequence
of fiery vowels antagonisms between consonants loud
and escalated when there is no ladder to approach
the upper levels where one of these Monday just may
enter the serenity of a following Tuesday should it
be the case and the heavens they all preach about
the Rapture or Armageddon the triumphant final
all-day of existence and time make their abrupt
appearance robed in the inevitable Jesus-flame
and all the tenderness we shared the sorrowing and
grief for the celestially clad whom we offered to the Holy
burning and lip to lip the brim of tears from eyes
reddened by the everlasting instant fire-storm
it all stops as ever why this Monday the unending

09-14-20

FIRST LOVE

folding sheets after school what they didn't tell you
adverse and flip the boy-friend from across town
the Rio Grande was on his back you listened
for the inter-com to tell you to stop both of you
from this distance the point seems poorly spent
however stolen love the kisses sealed were meant
but fear of flying and hanging on to pedestals
earth the constant darkness next days contained
all that jabbering in the hallway back-stabbing
adolescent rumor-mill were the shadows lingering
so inconvenient the promise not kept despite
phone-calls to the sheriff or mayor hello I am a
desperado on the hilt of light claiming just a few
minutes with Job's Daughter thin filaments of
thought broken illusions in snow-crusted alleys
bent back in supreme heat of endless kiss steam
rolling out from underneath car-hoods unkempt
as hair in a tornado before time takes its toll
and the future's rolled back eyelid unbearable as
all suns are before they blacken forever blotting
out the briefest of all moments budding green
paired hands groping to maintain tenderness shape
of the amorous contour when first ago we met

09-15-20

MARY LOU SONNET

this riddle was a surprise when the tenth wave fell
in one gold blaze the longing nor did Cynthia her
lapsing horns shiver in the wake as bodies are wont
into distant raging seas to fall their legions and fain
unknown the pale and fading members was life in
them still a blush or whispering in the brush come
the swift race of silent hours 'til this day we meet
not again but in sleep's weary trace a dream undone
the whole of time in its desperate inch the thumb that
blots with stifled ire memory of sweet abide the far
and lonely hills buried in their eternal winter now
so how then can we rejoin with compass or spell
that moment unawares when love us snatched
and the world outside its glass passed from the eye

09-16-20

THE AGE OF DISCOVERY

was then the spear shone bright its tip
to pierce the moon's dusty silver flank
and looking up espy the ghostly bark
afloat midst saffron suffused clouds
each the other's hand contained enigmas
shadows of undiscovered continents
and lip to lip undying love in fields
that spread past summer's furrowed noise
alas the wing its swoop conveyed lost
vowels an absence yet to come despair
the future's ruined carnival a fade and
unraveling of skies never to be seen

09-17-20

FOR JACK FOLEY ON THE OCCASION OF FRANK O'HARA

for the air that we breathe it must be the same
between jack-hammer drills and the smoke which
means the end of the world if not an abbreviated century
can almost mean what I say taking in the dun dusky hills
the slope between Parnassus and Vesuvio's next to
City Lights that is which is a career goal post for some
but failed for some character flaw by us and lest it
parade its Japanese syntax too loudly then sky encumbers
the souls passing through today with a mint wafer and
ginger-tea here have some as an accolade for the weary
eight decades are heavy but not so as the lapse of thought
can you still the orgone box long enough to hire a cab
so we two can get together at least one more time

09-17-20

SOME QUATRAINS ON
THE LOSS OF SUMMER

myth moves its Latin vowel legend sifts its grains
automotive reverie within cycles of unseen heat
bee swarms cluster in vitreous air grasshoppers
clamber on green blades in a tenuous ballet of

unencumbered grace of volatile flitting wings
the comma delta and asterisk the apostrophe
that embraces life's frail definition the screen
that divides *this* from *that* in a puzzling metaphysics

arms that cling to the void a body might have been
racing furrows to their harsh decline ant and
midge the violent sun blacken with destiny
tropes of passion perspiration and longing doubt

the mainstay of wind the swirling Caucasus of cloud
the edges of the universe infirm peninsulas of gas
the conjugated roar of silence in the solar homophone
each ear a film the unremembered verse of words

the loudest is the diphthong lodged in brick and leaf
followed by honeyed lesions the rumored vows
lovers make in their senseless disrobing thought
sundered by distances only planets understand

flailing orbs moon drifts of aspirin colored seas
noon when only statues hear the great catastrophes
future brings the riot of accident and glassy tragedies
too soon unborn too late revived the phraseology

of drugstore intensity and manic underhand
bound by ropes of flame invisible smokes archaic
lips that dampen the fevers of disbelief even as
fluttering lids the eye unbinds and leads into arcane

shelves where pages whiten their antiquity and
pressing prints of thumb and mind all else dissolves
but she in her skirts of swirling mystery and ore
the gold she frames in night's confounded lamp

excised photographs hieroglyphs of obscure dialect
was never meant to last love's fragile eternity
and nervously you ask does oblivion wear a smile
or is it vanished long gone into *time's* unending tomb ?

09-17-20

A SONNET

the sky the frame the death the stool
fields feet the greater numbness on high
delved and plunged the sea no more its inch
mind flung the singled thought a fast emits

winches pulled hoist rammed into ropes
twined gnarled and ivy stung the bee-swarm
a scope the barred metal lesser than red a
quarter of white twice the size of azure

why is there might ask the ploy a face fleet
as featured each is the other which is when
words don't mean only sounds the bric-a-brac
street the brick and plover rinsing time's bend

just look her blush the heightened near the eye
switching code a longing no longer lasts its *end*

09-19-20

EVEN ZEUS OF THE NETHER WORLD
AND DREAD PERSEPHONE

cut in half time no longer flies and quartered
by the amount of silver gone the moon itself retires
sky no longer holds most of the universe as we know it
a blade of grass is the weight of memory and no more
hearts are bled in verse of tectonic scales a vision

that takes in death's missing red corpuscles or
a serpent wrapped around the waist of a goddess
whose hallucinatory reduction is a dream of wasps
air fills with the *Invisible* ! ear resounds with what
has no echo and specters of our former selves
gesture and totem of a mythic refrain lost in egos
what are we but fossils of dew or the webbing
of unexpressed thought the fading of bright
in the noon-day of eternal time when for a fleeting
instant like negatives on a photographic plate
we became shadows of light statues of a quickened
immobility husks in search of wings to fly into
the maze of dust and sun the great darkening
in the brief afternoon of love the knee and brow
knit into the furrow where Persephone went lost
and you as well like her a phantom wraith whom
I can never again turn inside out in fierce oblivion

09-20-20

SOME HITHERTO UNDISCOVERED EPIC LINES

let us then to the stormy shores of Ilion
now gravid and tumescent the southern skies
and heap high the warriors' bones the blanched
on beaches strife-worn with care the plenitude
and size of red the coruscating hue of Mars
and then to heights the drowsy cloud implore
us to esteem the lost and forgotten the fog-eaten
stores of rock-hewn statues face down in the mire
was once this a place renowned a citadel a
bulwark to fend off flame and ire the foot
misplaces steps on weary gravel rounds wheels
alone cannot ascend and lightning distances
a poem requires to sound its second verses
its shattered vowels its accents brought down
to benches where reams of epic unwritten stale
words but noise the ears replete with darkness
the vagrant echo no crevice but hidden blood
shields and bucklers greaves and broken spear
what gods to whom we tend our palms upwards
glazed and jacked to peaks none can discern bring
to lasting sleep the fraught ends of this fractured
voice a leaf night-wept alone long lost in depths
such was thought these thin blue spiral spheres
gone like the smoke of all forgotten loves

09-20-20

TWO SMALL POEMS

(a)

the secret child
the beliefs I never
held publicized
but never owned
the poet I yearned
to be but words
I could not unravel
the trust I held
in sounds alone

utter the simple
vowels and breathe
the deaths I die

(b)

Más pesadilla que sueño
mas lejos todavía la luz
de la otra la primera vida
no más los poetas conocen
las verdades escondidas
en las hojas que duermen
bajo un cielo sin luna
¡ no más los poetas !

09-20-20

SUFFER THEM TO SURVIVE THEIR WARLIKE DEEDS

in the leaves that sleep under a moonless sky
seek we dream-speech quandaries and enigmas
left alone to die the many beyond our grasp
if dust and the uncountable grass and stars
the distant and instantaneous mean anything
if what we sense falling into the nocturnal depth
is merely nothing the blank overture to oblivion
then why do start at the new-found light dawn bears
as a vain torch to show the way to noon and its
statues and migraines and faltering ignition
finds us then a wary hour a supposition of loss
beyond the margins of the known world as space
itself withdraws its cards shrinking its tabulation
by at least as many zeroes as can fit the errant
thumb the aim and chasuble of the mechanic
who thinks to fix the tire or repair the hood
even as the celestial bowers flood with nemesis
the brooding black lamp that hovers over fate
a man as many men as are encountered daily
what are they but insects scouring a surface
in search for the millet grain the fallen crumb
bread and milk and the Parnassian glare of hope
does then the burden of memory the illusory
paradises of the bright day when and the joys
a rapture of summers wasted in a single second
face down in the humus and mulch of despair
where is the conduit that requires nothing of

history nor volumes of unfettered verse and tone
what is it standing on this corner we are expecting
is it to see falling from a cloud in golden raiment
the very angel snub-nosed and proud of love
to embrace the great emptiness of his wing-span
and in trance revive the enormous error of the mirror
another day another day another day the petty ruins
the car-park and the asylum where buffalo-ghosts
roam silently maddened by the lack of corners
earth is out of spin and floods and flames reign
nothing else moors on the shattered wharf
we look to the abandoned lawns and to echoes
hills of an idyllic west now devoured by the porphyry
of shadows trees of longing loneliness and absence
leaves that sleep beneath a moonless sky

09-21-20

HIC NEMUS ARCANUM

virulent altars overburdened with grief
a long smoking gone into dusky phrases
no ear can catch unless by stealth in sleep
the vow to make shore by midnight
hatched in ovoid dreams star-spent by
age undone memories entwined like laces
no hand can tie the spurious moment
aggravated by unknown light rendered
to the mourning hills their futile colors
can we then subservient to the divine sign
a mystery discern rapturous the bright
of a day inserted between tombstones and
the privilege to see beyond the roaming
ships the scuttled oars the prayers silently
when the sea comes rushing unspoken thoughts
a poem half undone the wind-sacks spilled
open at last the arcane wood tangled leaves
spears of invisibility the heart scour for a
truth to be whole not spurned by the fates
sisters at their wheel spinning tales about
us doomed mortals lost in dark gyres
you and I pronouns barely pronounced
released from laws of sound and returned
to depths where roots and vowels contend
with the fractured consonants of *silence*

the *echo* stones make waking up

09-22-20

SOME SONNETS ON THE SUBJECT OF POETRY

and varied with gold the raiment sewn
as skies do plunge from the unseen crater
so the bodies worn with time and no more
fit the rags now clad and slipped from shoulders
to the bone weary and come the dusky glow
of a following if there is one day the sloping
east of the horizon dipped into vats of time
darkness rears its unshaped density the glories
of once now fade the fray of verses known
a pallid echo a palinode in the ear of stone
would weep did eyes have strength and now
solemn the distance rings its tolling call
empty thoughts no more their weight sustain
slip from memory the vowels of fallen leaves

we were once those small soundings in green
voices calling out from a mythic upon a time
blood thinned and sun's shafts spread anon
languages of trill and web unheard rounds
of noise and dust the fabulous rushing seas
poet is a fragment of memory a writing is
to try to recall longing the whatever so pale
the fragility of actually the cosmos a whole
that cannot be pieced together by its parts
a poet is a fictive shadow summoning from
sleep dream sequences syllables of a light
dimly perceived as through water rushing
behind glass the specters of the many dead
who are the breath of his frail life the poet

can never have back the flood of fractions
consonants as varied as the trouble to recall
the pronouns they resembled the antiquities
in a single vocable etched in the sand of hearing
an enormous field of grass and dew and roaring
dawn's early digits tipped roseate the struggle
to restrain the horses of invention the swart
and mighty steeds hauling inveterate the ancient
black sun toward its pilloried noon insufferable
ruin of statue and temple and mimic of speech
poet as oracle or bleeding shaft or heart crowned
with the tragic grief of wreathes tonic accent
the flush tide undertow pulling away shadows
faint pronouns evocations of longing echoes

so this is what a poem comes down to its rock
and rush its plaint and substantive of zeroes
the unfinished never begun of sounds yearning
for meaning the subterranean cleft where shards
and splinters enigmas of dark splendors the way
of saying you were there too poet stunned what

a thing to be and radiance in the shimmering
morn and sudden hills the cliffs and dangers
nothing lasts it all goes into phonetic decay
weeping the unguarded moment when the child
the poet infant the abracadabra of illusion's love
poet whittled air resonance of distances too far
shapeless the planetary origins of poetry not
to ask to receive dumbly the mute ears of rumor

the deafened eye of poetry the lesions in tone
the phrases carved on the backside of an unseen
sprite vagabond tombstones paths of dejection
nowhere going by noon the middle of a statue
of the sea which is the death of the poem the
insouciant directionless wind storm the polity
of alphabets without beginning or merely
an end to everything that can be heard alive
dusky dusty mountains too far to reach by night
and rest the body in its death between space
and universal time nothingness evidence of poem
and recitations in the void by deities spawned
before language which is the poem in its raw
ineffable leafing bracketed by two darknesses

09-23-20

NIGHT AND THE DREAM-SCATTERING STARS

and so into the dark leafing afterworld
thoughts gone astray like petroleum evaporating
in a void which is greater than its perpetual inch
fossils of air tombs of wind the wounded atmosphere
light that has been cancelled before it starts raying
across the infinitude of moons circling a paraphrase
of monotonous rebirths among the pronominal
beings of disorder and masquerade each the other
of its mirror-self and then you as well as I perform
in the midnight sequence of world-play when
dissent and oracle contend for the perfect vowel
mountain peaks and hamadryads and leaping fauns
a mythic backdrop of wordless ignition—the mind
in its effort to finalize a persona a dreaming
utterly shadow-form going through the motions
of the everyday two hands to the left a foot to the right
perambulating as if in love and reciting from
a script written in cuneiform the verses first and
only of a poem invented by chance by one bent on praise
you or I which name will it be and the excursus
of the phenomenal and the multitudinous cinema
flicker-ending its tags of insouciant image-meal
do we then appeal to the invisible unnamed gods
who govern the reckless fates as if to alter
the latitudes of time and us the recondite souls
never asked to be born but induced into play-acting
the informal roles assigned to this ego and that
I know it's winding down it has nowhere left to go
the turn in the road is illusory the pages in the book
are unnumbered the sleep at the end of the wheel
the tattered leaf the sundered blade of grass
longing and memory the notches on an unseen branch
truncated and tossed into a ditch forgotten
come hour's end and the furniture burning
and the sermon of the Buddha on and on

09-24-20

WE ARE LIKE CREATURES WHO SEE THE SUN !

indefinable adjectives that qualify nothing
beside them we stand neither to affirm
or deny the very existence we assume
ours is the martial chariot hurtling from
the stars into this impeded noon of black
rays the very sun a sound a homophone
an inverse proportion to the darkness
welling up around our knees come mid-
afternoon when we consult the reading room
for a reference a clue a vowel a link to
something other than this entanglement
words without meaning heights and labor
the terror of going to sleep again the verse
memorized for class that we cannot translate
is it horse uphill and the grassy knolls where
Pan plans to destroy is it a vehicle or cart
bearing the humus of the dead into earth's
entrails we finger delusions with these letters
that go cursive and then the moon too that
hyaline infirmity upended in the late sky
when reason and its phonology hold sway
no more the mad man who dwells within
the insane proclivity to end the construction
relative clause postulates verbal delusions
the *if only but* and withstand details of rumor
the indelicacies of discovering in the chase
Diana in her pool what is that but death
the mistaken onlooker do we design other
endings tags and film clips and the walls
of Troy seized by an epilepsy tottering
brick and mortar the eye blinded shifting
into its red debacle the illicit love affair
the sentence the riddle of syntax paraphrase
of opulent syllables widening into a cycle
of heavens and those irritable deities and spoons
cleansing the stables and then what is the sense
of nightfall of iridescent distances annihilation
hand over hand the waves plunge deeper
into the abyss Nemesis and the debate about
the after-world located on the outskirts
and the grave western hills dun and vanishing

09-25-20

AN EARLY AUTUMN WALKS THE LAND

basking in the lake of advance
what is the thrill that comes second
given to grief the overwhelming life
in the leaves and the breezes monthly
what event is this dying now this
coming to terms in the peninsula
I know a division of sand an epithet
do words muster their incongruencies
to matter if only sounds and a hand
held to the light pointing clouds
burst in last summer's array
fastly coming home with one's twin
a shadow at a time the block of stone
to ponder is the eye's cinema
turning as skies do the eternal bend
a frisking the pockets an azure metal
flipped the disk and faces glow
appearing between reeds and music
grass and the everlasting finger
among it the phrase that darkens

09-25-25

IF TROUBLE IS MUTE WHAT
IS THE CONSEQUENCE

where is the center if not in the head ?
then space consists only of margins
which of the wind's seven directions
is the straight one that *leads*
if only the post card had been written
at a different time and place
you might not have died so mysteriously
as it is the evidence is in ink and red
the phrases predictable and longing
the whisk-broom of the avatars
like the vision you had of the 4th dimension
time traveler and moon-blot
a calendar at a time you reversed
the focus from lead to fire
now it's the end of still another month
fingertips and sand-paper the sky
what illumines is not the distant light
but the within where the soul
does battle with the embodied
I have learned to live on the edges
of the leaf the darkening that issues
from memory

09-26-20

THE AGGRAVATIONS OF HARMONY

(a)

words to pick from a field undone
blooms and petals the month sorts out
like days that have never been a wind
a wall a phrase snatched from the crowd

sounds that drill the invisible for more
echoes of echoing distances rock and leaf
mythologies of the unrisen sun the shadow
of light that blackens the reaching hand

vowel you repeat consonant you destroy
oracle of sleep the tangled verbiage like
a statue half-shaped from the mind's
quarry dust of noon hammer and ploy

grief's the issue the longing from afar
the never understood and raveled dark

(b)

what is the danger of the doubled sun
or the seascape that rushes past the knees
a picture is just a window a woven color
staggered in the passing light of time

twice the distance from thumb to eye
life as it unwinds in its spirit-house
troubling destiny in rolling dice
a battlefield of elbow and reckless words

you name it the ends are never quite
and however much the hill destroys
the poem it describes the gravel of the sky
falling stars twins parted by a hair

antiquities and harmonious descants
longing for the home buried in the wound

09-26-20

ORPHIC

(i)

you are the man who unknown
to himself is already the other
the inside-out of the diapason
thrilling to listen to the last note

the man who writes the poem
as if it were the unheard legend
of the rock and the nymph rills
a score for air and budding leaf

the man who you are is yet to be
a fixed person with a mask that
does not fit as it does the man
in the mirror the unrecognized

still you fall in love over and over
with what you lose repeatedly

(ii)

the exact is who she never was
stepping surfaces that don't exist
hair and brow the parted moon
her luster's backside broken crown

hamadryad or cliff-side fossil her
pronoun her frail display a shadow
weaving between vowels like running
water and wavers in declining sun

possessed by none and shudders
sleeping thongs the densest part
what shape she had shares with leaf
the hidden speech the missing sheaf

cling me to the riven rock she cries
losing grip a wraith of absent light

(iii)

so claim the two a music never heard
the rushing knees that absolve misery
backwards learned to seek no more
the shaking finger the sundered moss

this poem has nothing left to read
a lesson of shattered syllables the
betrayed sound the unreturned echo
in the key of delta the long and lost

so be you Orpheus or hap what may
your lyre's unstrung your lip's split

from grief your weeping is an ear
drained of sleep and night's revenge

sing no more the plucked branch
your head's a reflection in the flood

        (iv)
the tiny white hands are Mary Lou
who summons calling back from air
the darkening whorls of eventide
the carillon in her deafened ear

the witless corn in its autumn field
the frost about to gain its dominion
over unseen continents and above
all the plenitude of absent light

the decoration of an empty room
where untended beds await rest-
lessly phantom lovers who were
but silhouettes on the moving wall

all passes in a blade of summer grass
like the faint echo of two white hands

09-27-20

PAEAN TO THE SUN

who is the sun on this immortal day ?
does a hospital bed him contain
or railings made of mercury and brass ?
who has written these unnumbered verses
on the paving stone of our necropolis ?
what jabbering and automotive silence
what ears drained of ether and minds
toppled by a whetstone's curvature
am I the one with the steering wheel
that drives the blade into its Guanajuato ?
there is thirteen death and months to fell
before the grassy moon shapes its ellipse
against the mountain's absent pearl
there are wonders in a single vowel
and terror of the sigma sounded loud
who is the patient in the recovered planet
who yells night and day for more ice cream ?
a god he must needs be in oaken livery
a stone a peal of light a diphthong
waiting for its release a simple step
taken the wrong way up a cigarette and its girl
for once we know nothing well and climb

around the leaf's adolescent echo
smaller than the constellation *yesterday*
greater than the isotope of sleep

09-27-20

THE UNDISCOVERED TEXT

windows are a catastrophe in the making
so says the divine Archer aloft on his two-wheeled
chariot driving through storms of one-syllable poems
the doorway has a lintel of quicksilver
no one gets past the first of twenty signals
red blink blink blink followed by a semaphore
code of illustrated pages from the Book of Job
twice we called but there was only a hum
the bees of antiquity were at work in the slums of air
nowhere is there a capability of light greater
than in the inch of humus gathering around
the fallen shade of Achilles whose youth
was spent in the marble seas of memory
what is now a simple equation between vowel and vowel
a blade of grass a surfeit of gravel a sky
lowering its texture of filmed cloud-bursts
none of this has relevance the world is aflame
cattle have revoked their biblical passage
a mountain that was not here yesterday
and in Latin now overwhelms the port
what is it we don't *get* ?
tomorrow is an impossible digit of asbestos
the free-fall of angels corrupted by methane
an insistence on the irreversibility of matter
the spear sobs as it proves its crimson point
cigarettes manifest mysteriously in the fingers
of girls whose roseate features dissolve in smoke
the world is aflame and people only seem to
hear the mutation of consonants in their migraine
can there only be one way back ?
windows are a catastrophe in the making

09-28-20

FIVE NEW SONNETS

(i)

they plied the tufts with clouds of ore
reddish metallic sky Zeus loves to play
mountain scores with tops of ire and spleen
when readied for gore the troops sally
from the Northern gate into the hoar
why's the plaintive moan the ear dreads
to fill the clashing unseen dividends of
iron and brass a shield it splits the universe
between the quick and the dead rusty
piles upended on ant-heaps the move
to victory lost in the grime and spit whose
mother's son tender so sweet his remains
a face and hair two eyes rolled back
to look at heaven's fixed inch of time

(ii)

for the eternity of one hundred million kalpas
I would not trade this moment of light this
summer contained in the breadth of voice
hidden in the leaf the stone that sits road-side
the swimming hole whose depths I searched
for the love of a lifetime these eternities notched
in the inch of bark on the willow tree are
as nothing to the instant when unawares I unearthed
the poetic wars of antiquity the fiercest of
all struggles of Aphrodite and her paramours
the indelicacies yet ever so gorgeous of holy
infidelity in hexameters the length of space
how many nights buried in the soul of Achilles
do I now withstand the deaths of these eternities ?

(iii)

two fingers to the left of light the display
of all the dead stars like immobile fireflies
suspended against the moving screen
youth it says in duplicate above the shaving
mirror the remembered hand the eulogy
for each of the still uncounted gone those
whose lives went unnoticed in the ambulance
and who of disabled fate still struggled
to revive the numbers two or three efforts
to recapture the painful loss of consciousness
the hour the virus ate the nerve and bright
the swiftly dashing sun turned night-black
and all the noons of a heroic meter to shade
turned swallowing *noise* in its swift silence

(iv)

to paraphrase the asterisk and ivy the red
moon and the clauses that exclude space

from its dominion and ankle deep in terror
history itself loosens its spears and slings
the toss of a diphthong the turn of the die
wheels over-run by their own direction and
speed of loss multiplied by primeval grief
come on it's all over the road has no place
to go the poets in their bewilderment have
their last line erased and stand accused before
silence of their cliff and duplicity the frosts
of timeless night the envy of petty gods
whose job is to ruin stairs and wells the dot
that punctuates the infirm sky is ever gone !

(v)

so quick the dumb began their statuary
and speech of knives and dreaded consonants
each is noon the time to die the highest light
in the frozen sky turns black before the eye
come fix the palinode the grace note the choir
in its decibel of endless silence and hasten
to reward the minions buried in a flake of snow
the mangled names of ancient poetry the hand
designed to thwart the heavens and cloud
of theaters the silhouettes parade their domes
will ever this sequence end or words mean
more than what they sound will vowels
retrace the threads of echo to the darkness
of the stone the leaf and grass of sleep ?

09-29-20

WATCHING THE FIRST PRESIDENTIAL DEBATE 2020

the length it takes the inch to form its mile
the eloquence of living in the last breath
before the cymbals of eternity still the ear
why is the voice torn from the leaf
and the stone made to weep in its maelstrom
of grass and light and what is it the cathedral
of trees has to say to the running stream
the dignity of man is elusive and the gods
who have repeatedly withdrawn their support
who is the shadow plugged into the wall ?
what is the person inside the mask trying
to say in order to get out and the musk of sleep
and the thrust of waking on the mirror's left side
am I that face am I that trembling hand
am I that imposition on gravity ?
the passing years gone up in smoke
the cigarette and the girl and the drug store

the small digits of reference and error
the glass that exists between reflections stained
by the actors' incoherent lines and you know what
it's over the lawn in its brown decrepitude
the planet in its whirligig ellipse out of control
mayhem of the poem that cannot begin and
what's more the oval and the square and the
famous rectilinear attitude of the sophists
you ask why today ? why is the syllabus
of western history set on fire
why do the museums gather in their bones
and talking and talking nonsense the statues
in their polite marble gone mad because their noon
with its perpetual blackening sun will not arrive
I am of grief the component most likely to
and you willy-nilly on the sidelines
tumbling shadows among the dandelions
I remember the once when tight and tall
you made a passage for the waters of night
and spoke with all the angularity of the prophets
gone ! the whisk broom and fly swatter
the bla bla bla of words in their vain sonority
let's take a drive over the cliff
the mangled heavens look down on us
pitying our inability to resurrect the vowels
in their primal order and left to babble
clutching our electronic devices in a swoon
let it go ! there's only so much air left breathe
into the woods for one last meditation
highways of echo ! brevity of space !
the little spotted deer that peer from the other side
in their great liquid eyes a shattered universe
pivots silently pivots silently at last

09-30-20

GLOBAL WARMING BLUES

the highest degree is very cloudy and heat
has its volumes torn from the leaf a speaking
in monograms that leave no trace a future
in the vacuum of vowels and the indecent gesture
of statues aching to simply feel the stroke of noon
digital emotions thumbs of desire inches left to breathe
spawning new universes as the old one tilts
past the poorly projected moon in its diaphragm
the forests are burning into perpetuity the small
birds owls and terns and gulls looking for the seas
that were evacuated last night and the Bull-Roarer
of civilization and progress dumb estimates
of what next year will be like when there are no
years left to count and how the ice flows !
the subcutaneous Morse code has forgotten its Esperanto
under each fingernail the sinister brown excrescence
of cancer or HIV proceed with minute hexameters
how many are the statistically dead today ?
an erroneous number the equivalent of India
where the raga keeps its insane and infinite drone
playing in the isolation units and on and on
look ! the sky has precisely two disks left
one for the backside of angels and the other for
the forgotten Olympians muddling in Alzheimer's daze
it is time for the Mayo Clinic to fold up its aprons
the mutant buffalo of the park with their crazy red eyes
are about to burst out of their pens to reclaim
for the Ojibway the spirit world that hovers just
centimeters above the Freudian dream surface
but the Flames ! Paradise has been consumed twice
the inhabitants of Purgatory herded into the mountain
where the destination of man is reduced to small
squiggles in cuneiform *italics* the breviary of hate
fever is the norm ! epistles to Barons and Popes
yet nothing is done and inactivity is the heights!
remember as children how we played eventides
waiting for the amazing map of stars to rise
they're gone ! blindness and political expediency
and there's just one more thing
how I hate to see that evening sun go down

10-01-20

GOING TO THE MOVIES WITH MARY LOU

don't remember a thing of what we saw
watching sawdust cowboys riding imaginary horses
around a neon bend holding hands blindfolded
intricacies of railroad plots and beaches where
famous movie-stars squabble before the Japanese attack
pouring rain from manufactured clouds into a musical
without any instruments just absent voices
too loud to distinguish the vowels and chicanery
about hayrides and swooning Latin Lotharios
hair piece of black shellac and moonshine
did we ever know how it ended ? a lexicon
of riddled mountains and an infernal hour of bliss
sitting in the dark of the famous lost planet
hoodoo monosyllables in one brain and out the
other lip-synching the song about the pyramids
was it a comedy ? were there battleships waiting
to be imbellished at the corner of Hollywood and Vine ?
and Ravel's Bolero ? it's all about high-school
infinite monotony of four years going steady
soon it will be the future a graveyard with
paper poppies and opium eating Lovers
imported from Nagasaki after the blast
as for the invention of the telephone and the miniscule
orchestra inside it playing Rimsky-Korsakov's
Scheherazade for days on end and the hills
governed by remote control how many decades
of filmed snowfall and the diameters of language
scribbled in the very first line of the Poem
exegesis and dialectic of longing the far-off and
haunting reminiscences was that how it started
and what happened in the middle and rhymes
and meter and making each diphthong count as two
after-school mooning in the library stacks
where the Roman Empire fell and thousands of
philandering and stolen kisses what an event
sound-track of mock Cecil B DeMille thunder
Ben Hur and the apostles and the deaths in the catacombs
and the Robe spread out for the dice & half-undressed
Cleopatras with thick indigo junk around the eyes
love me forever ! is it a wonder the show never ended
film loop and miles of synthetic antiquity
heaven in a seraphic burst of tinsel-chorales
too soon the future will have come and gone and the spare
obituaries of faces who have passed diminished
in a series of consonant clusters euphemisms
and doctored legends about Circe and Penelope
rhetoric and labyrinth of unrepeatable vows
once in a lifetime ! sitting there in night-atmosphere
boyfriend and girlfriend centuries in the making
clasped in the dark swath of infinity called oblivion

10-02-20

MOPSUS

simulated arms he ties to the Styx boarding
a passage that takes an instant before infinity
takes over with its holy oaks and saplings
hears nothing of the voice trapped in the branch
with its dialects of leaves and sounding a rumble
the parched skies break in triplicates a cloud
for each eye that has lost memory of the day
so we too in the park darkening sense the shade
that comes like a wave over youth and destroys
all in the following breach of light and now hear
the high unmodulated piping of the boatman
careens from the shore rippling stale waters
do faces plunge and arms look the other way
sweet constancy was of the moment now bodies
ravaged by time's cruel promise and dip the oars
into the sluggish flow listening for ice to come
into being and the heaving hoary distances
must this hour and when the reading volume
lifts its accent and the terrible syllable shifts
into red gear the trumpeting planet in the ear
forever cancels sleep were night not so stolen
the starry welkin amassed to the far right
in a corner where lamps are forbidden you can
almost understand the why of everything else

10-02-20

TODAS LAS LENGUAS POSIBLES
para john m bennett

the digits and shelves and discarded gloves
pantomime of disorder and sorrow mapped
in small vocalic zones called nemesis until
tomorrow everything was OK or at least
registers in the red key and sulfate and other
like diseases the *gesta romana* trumpeting
in the hillsides where guerilla warfare
distributed according to dialect and speaking
of statues the first of their kind moving
mysteriously across the spectrum of human
speech diglossia backwards tongue flaps
total phonetic disorder of the human condition
when darkness begins to echo irreversible
the tiny rumors midges squalls ants ticks
gestures of facial corruption and always
backhanded muffled glottological mayhem
when shoulder envies knee and grief and high
in the bright summer of a sun gone black
as pitch tone and accent of sibyline discord

disoriented alignment of false consonants
lunar and retroflex at the same time how is
the verb to be and how is it not and fictions
of meter and the unheard ear musically deaf
give us back the rhyme of leaf shaping air
hazard of the welkin as it plunges once again
and didn't you notice it too the riverrun
twice over in the paragraph about heat
the logic of cycles and new forms of hand
yearning for ancient hill chords underbrush
cinder and tilt until modernity sparks anew
in books unpaginated and disposable why
read any more why enter discourse analysis
semantic fragmentation of thought and sleep
is about to dream-talk and clouds seamless
and abrupt where the mansion of azure
out of context and near the end of the start
the summit where and why the easiest is
to forget to sound to utter anything a word
is a puff of breath or two a click of the teeth
a rattle in the throat gargling suppositions
of meaning and intent the eye gone wild
in the hemisphere of rope and come night
the whistle in the grass the length of memory
the small allotment of enigma to the dead
who emerge from time to time in the south
where unused spears pile up and rust and
the oblique case-form of unknown nouns
what is it we want to say and hear who is
the one who should be formulating glyphs
years go by and the passage the dusky ire
the flattened extension of mortality longing
buried deep in the unsounded vowel

10-03-20

TWO INEFFABLE SONNETS
"a fricção delicada do silêncio contra o silêncio"
Clarice Lispector, A Maçã no escuro

(a)

and long by far the cliff from sea removed the space
immemorable between thumb and index the shadow
five inches thick that extends the crossbow of its intent
across the mere and doubled hour no end in sight
the ear plunged drastic into vowels unheard and
lightless the unmirrored depths where struggle
souls with Stygian ropes and held back fast the body's
tight shirt the shoulders drizzled in brine the first
to hold anchor to the fist the dreaming a wary
voice without command in a secret Latin expunges
from oblivion the treasured consonant of breath
delusions that love's grasses loosened and the gravel
intricate with insect labyrinths a choice to heighten
or merely to conjecture the delicate frictions of silence

(b)

illusive heat of summer's long last frame a distance
too narrow to comprehend even as the moon's twenty-seven
brides withstand the dialogue of ellipse and pelf
what raiment of intense burning the skin alone retains
and the order of stars the number of meters betrayed
in the poem's insouciant doctrine of grief and travail
innocent losses grass and winding sheet mournings
that weep against dawn's glassy blaze these untruths
written in dew and transferred to the language of oracles
do submit the quarrels of sky and infinity and sleep
which is the reef that lifts the sea from its monocle and
years compress in the tiny fix of dying surrounded
even as gods smoking and fainting the pavement stain
what century is so blind what hour so infinitely gone ?

10-04-20

N*A*P*O*S*P*O*T*L*A*N

I woke and saw a place call *Napospotlan*
not seen before its motels and snowy peaks
a highway of running ink and cactus flowers
budding red the sky its livid hue of mornings
uncounted stained that mounted grieving
for days that will be no more decoys of joy
freighted with hooded shouts silver masks
that decorate distant walls and voices as
if booming from deep-bottomed wells
mercurial ascent of tutelary planets and
solar homophones loud in the sheltered ear
how often have I been and how often doomed
to not return the invention of memory the evening
and fix of oblivion on parallel courses through
a dream-scape of tortured hyacinth and willow
hands in search of their own voices and leaves
whose darkening slender shapes evoke a past
that could only be heard but never seen a light
that echoed its own shadow in gleaming glass
Napospotlan ! inverted pyramids underground
rivers kingdoms of mescal and pulque where
afternoons last for years immersed in trance
diglossia of ancient kings consecrated vowels
rising accent of priests hidden in vast drums
tom-tom code finger-rings large as consonants
of drill and denim and the aching forsaken
myth of the dying who own the great south
mountains and weirs and trampled growth
amazing fruit that drops from clouds and tears
more than in abundance bright ambulances
that fly through cliffs and defiles bearing
the gifts of immortality and amnesia –
Napospotlan ! the life immemorial of grass
and maps that repeat themselves on display
to have never been and yet recall everything !
I know the route as it decays phonetically
the dust and dusk of syllables that vanish
no sooner sounded and the oracular Eye
of statues erected to last a single noon
will ever be the youth of myrmidons ?
fluctuations of time so dense the reverse
is what we mean when we learn to talk
high on rooftops of volcanic ash and laundry
ropes and dark-skinned nurse maids and
a presidential palace made of sugar-skulls
Napospotlan ! my childhood of floating gardens
the last and first and of aphasic destiny
alone with my only twin inverse and solo
dread hemispheres of nativity and sorrow
thirteen-death and seventy two years !

10-05-20

THE INSTABILITY OF LIGHT

obscure the cloud that hangs the day's torments
not as in a dream statues have in the course of
the unknown hour but the end of friction and gravity
even as ascending the mortal breathes its last release
reckless waves the freighted sea of dangers to
the literal shores of mankind a wasting of all matter
the drowned and of puerperal fever the ones
of the gone dominion the sabbaticals of loss
what memory there is of the passing flame the beams
and rays of a storied image rock and sandy vowels
plied upon the spatial warp at speeds of sleep
and intricacies labyrinthine of uncounted syllables
weeps absence and mourning in the ceaseless turn
the body takes plunging into oceans of fire
unseen the articles that surround the remoteness
mountains waking among the cognitive alphas
yet unbound the soul is left to wander in gaping space
timorous stars trembling asterisms sparks
that punctuate the great instability of light
as yawning leaning leftward the aphasic brain
struggles to remember the day of gifts and love
the ornamental moment of birth the burning charge
the conjunctions that separate the *this* from *that*
small egos tracing with a damp finger constellations
of muted grass and leaves that yearn to speak
all that was felt so bright to be and nothing less
the dotted lines of eternity passing from the core
the roar and catastrophe of unending dark

10-06-20

PRESIDENT TRUMP TAKES OFF HIS MASK

makes me sad this country lives by peril
jeopardy and disease the awful each day
becomes is this wrong alive in this suffocating
and whelmed at the rudder of this Enterprise
cheek by jowl madder than whatever gleams
in the eye of each passing cloud or bent
the blade of every grass saddens mourning
the many-fold daily chimes tolling extra deaths
by the thousand you can buy cheaper than
sandpaper and the lot of mortal kind has
even less value sorrowing by the inch within
a magnifying lens the frame and fix the flux
of the diurnal pest yawning by mayhem tawdry
lesions like pearls of sun the cast of dye
the purplish apoplectic apocalyptic you can
guess the meaning of this verse a meter thinks
agent orange the blush that hues the cry
a sky lessened from view the naked blot
of pitch the blackened ivory knolls the hall
when even the girls and masked prey the
constant saddening drum hammers beating
a temple and the seas in their green shelves
is it the roaring wind in the statue's ear
yes a mound a heap of blustering effigy
call it the democratic rind and just as this
ends a day so what's to expect come
the morrow grieving dawn the red flush
fists and gore the triplicate and brightness
fades hills of distance world after words that
hollow endings implore don't they cry ?

10-06-20

TWO EXTRA SONNETS

i

such brightness he sends upon the waters
nor gleam so at noon the day's remote hills
as does the eye sporting with shadow and light
then does death run its course and hap fells

the many youth in chase and battle the weapons
that glinting fly into mid-air and streams of
sweat and gore their sheen apply the mottled
skin the gaping wound without contrition

into the underbrush fall the tainted bodies
and souls like winged midges take flight high
in such wise polluted streams smoke-choked
winds and cities in devastation lie beneath

Zeus' blanketed curse the world's coming end
and we watch stupefied this staged mystery play

ii

to speak in archaic and stress the vast unknown
and trace the crooked silver rills of memory
using verdant vowels and tongues that sing
the loud and sweetened canker sore the loss

and dread the mounting numbers that implore
yet none can count and fewer still recall the order
of the mind's first alphabet when rock and quill
great verses plied on the monumental night

stars do come and go and comets with blazing
tails and rituals of adversity and grief performed
when none are there to watch the lamenting
consonants stricken from the lists and plunge

into the abyss of man's own hand the shapeless
toss of errant seas and winds the infinitely gone

10-07-20

TWO MORTALITY SONNETS

a

everything happened and nothing happened
the goddess of speech in her shadowy brocades
and linen appeared but only as a sequence
of vanishing vowels sometime after midnight
the deaths the important ones tubercular mothers
cars on assignment to crash and the highways
often unseen the liquid ribbon running through
sleep adverse and unacquainted with day and
the enormous homophone of the sun darkening
we wagered with the wrong ones and walking
back into the park with its circular legends and
at odd angles the swings and slides until upside
down the grass and the sky beneath the grass
could we really have been there playing ?

b

air and its distilled vacancies the man define
as dying his elimination evokes a leaf a sobbing
and a stone startled by its road-side hour
such links as inform yet darkening suffixes
implore words to end and hyphenate the very
next stage somewhere between Tiryns and
the rocky shores of Ionia a philosopher will
step and plunge the stars once seen to heighten
a dazzle of sparks or a monumental firefly
this man you speak his hold infirm breath
in isotopic increments I knew him as you well
astride his horse of cloudy dreams turning gray
an apostle of the unspoken letter relief in toto
amaze that all remains as nothing in the winds

10-08-20

"MIGHTIEST AMONG THEM IN STYGIAN ARTS"

fishermen at the well the dirty faces of literature
foreboding the next wink of the constellations
will saddle the exit with hues and tones unknown
dipping feet into the shoals children that all will die
a laughter and cans of worms and the gasoline
that rainbows the muddy puddle by the house
where at night they bring extinct shadows
to perform rites sounding in algebraic whispers
the promises of a nether life reading texts
that no one has written and bongs and gongs
the basso profundo of a marked revelation
chanting the exhumed dittos of the passing night
clouds the shape of ink or sand and the dreams
of glass lifted into the nowhere of the galaxies
it is a girl-friend at first then an illicit drug
the mind takes on new forms the advance of number
to the extent that three is possible and the clock
that towers the shadowy vale how it lingers
absent of hands and the phases of Chronos lapsed
there is no score to sing no gladness in the bier
clasped to the whole of space the various souls
nodding soon lose all topography and name
longing how the leaf traces its size in the dark
which is the beautiful recitation of silence

10-08-20

ASPHODEL FIELDS

or waking the stones and expecting their thought
to go on through accolades of dust the sleep of time
an hour is not too much and the trees suddenly
taller more tranquil than before and the antiquity
resonant in the brooding leaves because the autumn
spell is in the azure and bountiful air yet shadows
also elongate the spirit that no body can contain wistful
as the notion seems to be reflecting back from glass
held against the provoking sun when midday becomes
the pulse of memory as soon as it is dissolved
from the frail numbers that held it in check for this
brief segment of atmosphere rumbling distances
portend the wake of clouds and the ritual of tiara
and drum-head spectral as moons in the afterworld
which is today the sliding silence of an archaic vowel
pronounced by statues abandoned in their park
there is no coming home nor an again of childhood
phrases and metonymy that linger breathing
as if to revive one of the multitudes who have gone
to join asphodels yellowing in their hidden fields

10-08-20

SOUTH WHERE THE DEAD

sunnyland the trees and lambent breezes
a sorrow refer to the archaic rock fragments
whose shadow cannot escape noon's immolation
abiding in recesses deep in memory's cliff
wounded by the false oracle of Parnassus
exquisite vowels dismissed from sound the highest
point where the sun's banner touches eternity
does Juno call forth the eastern winds ?
stillness and heat hold the fleet in a mirage
liquid content of oblivion and sails slack
against the mirror of air about to shatter
is this the day of mortal retribution ?
knee against knee and the depths of sleepers
unkempt in their hospital sheets and girdles
there is a window somewhere and birds that
fly circling bright with great wingspan and
there is a mountain on the other side of time
where the dead come to reckon the ruins of speech
had they but shoulder and brow to wreck
gazing forever south to the promised land
a drizzle of consonants that puzzle the ear
rumors of infinite phonetic disrepair
longing and grief they submit to the hours
that pass silently imitating the solar disk
to what end the human gambit notched
in the sublime and immense air that surrounds
none there are who can summon the Pronoun
the humiliation of ego and being the error
of miasma buried in the myth of light
who can touch the leaf without weeping ?
the head is a stone the hand is grass
summer ! breath and darkness

10-09-20

THE DEATH OF HYLAS

then there was all that name calling
back and forth rock to rock echo to echo
the endless silence and the explosion
of sound deep within the night of silence
motion itself a symptom of legend a simple
projection of thought mind's supple exercise
laying the head beside its stone the profound
stillness before the first blade of light
birth or rebirth in the tanneries of memory
lowing and suffocation second and third
moments when space yawning at its cavity
emerges between the unspoken syllables
conjecture of time as the vowels evolve
out of the cicatrix and reunion of the waters
huge yet unadorned the branches reaching
out and up from some unfelt origin a tree
a tranquility of semblances a spreading
out of the new found darkness into its afternoon
province of shadows and statues yearning
of matter to dispose of itself and lift high
into the unsearched empyrean for a shape
ideational content of air the pause and hiatus
before consciousness the bright ineffable
before and after of noise the section above
the limit of sky where thunder assumes
its oracle and booms crescendo of rumors
vague at first the ominous flashing beyond
the definitions and sleeping dense in folds
of ever more rapturous silences the spark
of the eye the floodgate of lamps widening
in the breadth of the measured inch of sound
recorded in the dormant ear a hissing of
values a wedge like a thumb impressed
in the new wax of the sun lifting now
its blazing allotment of ether bannered
subjunctive of the elemental verb of hours
revolving now on the spectral wheel that
rounds landscapes of the western hills horizons
of finger and grass and tumult of dust
about to burst into a cosmic fragment brighter
than the apocalyptic crash at the end of
things the nouns of catastrophe and their
puny adjectives whistling wildly in a music
of unbearable eternity that very instant
when childhood collides with death's reddening
fissure in the kaleidoscope of remembrances
slope and grade and defused number
when all becomes grief the unmeasured loss
the hand without shape the tongue of remorse
knee and shoulder capsized in an algebra
of totemic shifts and the finalized word

never pronounced buried in magma
of great forgotten hexameters
the Nymphs

10-10-20

THREE MORE ORPHICS

a

thy head flows and anon
thy hands their shadow seek
thy tongue an emblem in the dark
thy voice nothing left to speak

why raise the vowel to its pitch
why endeavor to alter the unfit
why seek the great unsought
these words are but for naught

twice or thrice the mind awakes
thrice is more than it can think
the fingers dabble in pure ink
these sounds are just mistakes

they're but statues consumed at noon
by the flaming sun-sphere's homophone

b

been to the netherworld nothing there
to drink but asbestos peeling on the walls
a flame three-tongued beast hell's maw
to greet the weary shadowless who crawl

has been here my Eurydice wide–justice
her etymon that turns to ignited vowels
have seen her shape and cried aloud
but turned around to lose her ever more

unfit to alter the paltry human score
abrasive nouns consonants that do not sound
harsh echoes that pass through solid rock
my music the single unsung note of sleep

archaic tongues silenced by this lament
tragedy in the leaf the shape of endless night

c

the Latin version has passed from memory
the Greeks sought to clarify the holes in space
the homonyms that stand for purity and death
buried in the undiscovered mountains of the west

strike out every other word erase the mere intent
blot from the early sky the youthful solar disk
go no farther than the unwritten script of clouds
below is never deep enough for the sleeping rock

a blaze in the first of twenty noises from afar
rumor of dust and immolated rays of light
heavens that exist between thumb and index
hell that is the canopy of everlasting night

I am but a singing head a lyric of liquid hair
a mind dissolved in a verse of rushing waters

10-11-20

JOE AND I ATTEND OUR FIRST FUNERAL HILLS AND RUSHING SUMMER AIRS INVOLVE THE UNSEEN GREENERY AND ITS INFIRMITY

the poisoned fruits of alchemy
the newt in the astrologer's eye
the text dumbfounded in its script
and the mirror's reversed sympathy
the wain that rumbles in the uppermost
Zephyrus that blows his ears out
Jupiter's raving winter tongue
that brings to mortals constant dread
this life unsure this world undone
illusions that prey on the unawares
love's distance in stormy echoes
vowels like empty rusted scabbards
the bruiting oracle of the stone
the grasses that flow over summer corpse
the rock upon which we twain sat
amazed at the forfeit of living breath
the body we glimpsed in its eternity
was it like us in drunken sleep
how would we ever wake ?
was *again* the next to nothingness
that took us hopefully to bed ?
what are thoughts but unkempt threads
the youth of pine the nodding breeze
the anklets worn by invisible deities
the scorn they pour on human mind

the gods in their prattle of the dense
this afternoon is eternal and forever
tomorrow is the hill we cannot climb
Brother ! who is that one unknown
who can never rise from his sheets ?
the teacher of the declined noun
the book of scribbled letters red
inks and plows and corn-yards wide
remoteness of thumb and compass
weights that manacle the air
the high-school from which we float
a grief of Latin panoplies
too soon we'll recognize the body
in each of us is dead
too soon from the cliff we'll part
and into that body swift descend

10-11-20

ADVAITA

as when the sun separates from itself
turning noon into countless replications of flame
divine beings stoned on light !
and the silence that exists inside the solar syllable
the immense explosion of unheard darkness
only intensifies the puzzle of duality and multiplicity
that seems to govern the expanding cosmos
if we are still in high-school enumerating coffins
as they glide mysterious by in front
of the immense blackboard where vowels
are conjugated for their likeness to breath and being
and time stands still on the nub of chalk
no hand has an understanding of itself
no shadow can walk backwards through its dictionary
no shouts of glee because the three o'clock bell
nothing of that just the sheer enormity
of doubt which is the future on its stilts and cranes
lifted enigmatically into the heavens where
Zeus in all his abracadabra falls from the pulpit
dividing the sound he makes crashing into hemispheres
of sleep and endlessness and yet and yet
we do exist for a brief half-second in the labyrinth
of unities and count as well as we can the trinities
that fall outside the non-dual pale the aboriginal
boomerang or butterfly the immensities of mind
becoming other than itself on the steep discourse
of metaphysics and annihilation the X Y and Z
of the cosmos obliterating its origins every second
it's not what you say but what you forget that matters
climbing the pyramids of the sun and moon

wearing your wrought-silver mask of Huītzilōpōchtli
which makes you invincible to that ninth grade rhetoric
that establishes footballs fields and land mines
for posterity // no it is the struggle with the number Two
the birth of duality you must disestablish in your
long ages-deep incline toward a day out of time
bric-a-brac of disunion gods with no faces
water that has no bottom letters out of sequence
pasted to an effigy of Eternal-Return and all that
leads to the monotone disjunction of space
remember when we played charades and
the girls mooning about with their redundancies
of facial make-up and hair-combs and the piano there
when you sat down and played *Heart and Soul*
you knew it was the end that there was no
other side to things no fission or fusion
that we were all already dead
bright integers lacking front or back
discounted from our own invisibility
it's not what you say but what you forget that matters

10-12-20

INDIA

birds with hands
red walls green poisons
city of the gods dust miasma
imperiled breath illusory lamps
suffixes without words
glorious cloud-script
mosques tattoos sanctuaries
loudness in statues
noon sculpted from henna
violent hair-do of mausoleums
elephants charging water
marble with leprosy
apocalyptic trees shaking
insect hordes in the market
fruit vacant of light
moon abscess and whips
eyes inverted corollas of hemp
Bang and opium perfume
unwritten histories of mud
one-thousand-fifty-six deities
all named Govinda
wandering forests
mountains with translucent wings
hummingbirds and demons
each with three hemispheres

arbitrary homophones of sky
rutilating horses of dawn
endless syllable humming
bees the size of dynamite
letters of diaphanous parrots
singing in stone threads
upended retroflex consonants
constant ignition of sound
the enormous nowhere of time
forty seven directions
coupled tongues of bats
caves without entrance
saliva the color of ink
everywhere is south
echo of the drizzling mind
sutures in the unseen body
troubled ears of rice
salvation without redemption
hills of phonetic turbulence
dialects of thunder
nirvana in the occluded thumbnail
thrones of one vowel only
decimated atmospheres of love
thrice holy evaporations
altars the length of memory
sheer incandescence
smoke and extinction
burning eternities of music
Radha Krishna
Radha Krishna
Radha Krishna

10-13-20

DEATH WATCH

houses inhabited by nomadic spirits
noon and living and wasted joys
the windows flood with white shadows
wherever memory has been forgotten
a jewel or a golden lotus sprout
emblems of oblivion and depth
all of space tossed back and forth
by deities that chatter like monkeys
today as on no day at all death
lifts pairs of palsied hands into
the lies of air the circumference of sky
reduced to its spare inch and automobiles
of gravity descend like a rain of frogs
pestilence and avarice are the dice of the day
perpetuity incarnate in the torn silk of the eyelid
hovering like a massacre of bees or
the tortured insect of light the atmosphere
and what it governs tumultuous as a consonant
of thunder misplaced in the grammar of omens
dissected corollas of the discarded echo
vowels plunging in a dichotomy of illusion
brains that think wheels are the square root of time
illness and profligate noises shatter shop windows
who walks in the labyrinth of horns
risks forever the ability to remember
a bird sent from the drinking cup of Zeus
telegraphs its orient in a haze of pitch
never mind the erased syllables of sleep
the dysfunctional foot the movement of ink
waters of abandonment like the cries
of the child left in the homophonic hills of the sun
no wonder death is dazed today has no hips
to circulate no maps to deviate the essence
is lunar the solar pronunciation has failed
give us hemp to hang the word
and to go on into the late afternoon burning
without smoke and the stairs where we linger
go neither up nor down and death
as always improper indecent yet gorgeous
soiled eyes and lips painted deep indigo
the lamps that stain death's cheeks
and to go on raving ?
monads of leaves whispering
sleep cannot be revived !

10-13-20

HISTORIA VERDADERA DE LA CONQUISTA

great cadavers of heat circulating
like unspoken romance dialects in the ivy
& to sleep in summer's ornate diphthong
yielding to the profound *ampersand*
woven into the nexus of eyelid and sight --
why go on piercing darkness with
Toltec lightning riding cordilleras that
differ from Spanish or Sanskrit as much as
distance diverges from the porphyry of longing ?
inversions of the horse and swart perspiration
armor soldered to glistening herculean frames
and the flotilla of imported hills charging surf
the whiteness of the outer rim the deep indigo
that is fatal to the eye the immensities of cobalt
even as its avenues sprawl into nopal underbrush
flowers fired from archaic muskets like troops
of cloud-elephants prepared to seize the continent
blinding whatever passes for light in the gloaming
boomerang and volcano and ninety-degree alcohol
when skies did battle with skies !
the ungovernable envelope of *siglo de oro*
with its plethora of misdirected synonyms
shepherds and avatars of lazar-house gods
the unique digit that transforms sound into space
echo after echo of an unheard Basque consonant
ready to detonate the lacerated backside of Cuba
the life of the ear and its golden assonance
in the rushing welter of oceans on the other side
of the perforated and pearly Lobe
ringing syllabic disunities in rock and moss
mufti and corduroy of the managerial knees
sequences of traffic racing the invisible storms of Tampico
where gun-runners and affidavits of bright toxicity
lounge half-drunk in the ravaged tropical greenery
saliva and boredom of the new ruling class
borrowed gypsum thoughts heaving mountain-peaks
dialects of Chapultepec childhoods the works
hobbling with Franciscan mountebanks from the Old Country
gringo hospice dereliction of the Carretera Panamericana
where it is always the summer of 1953 BCE
when the *twins* besieged the Popol Vuh motel
ransacking dust and brick the bath of fame inches
within the insect who bears History on its carapace
and corn fields planted with munitions and
the unending Communist Revolution of Cuauhtémoc
the motor buried deep in Xochimilco floral beds
water follows water into the reverse of the leaf
whose exhausting idiom divides night
into the multiple hemispheres of Oblivion

10-14-20

TOMB OF THE POET

designations of light and dust
the motor behind each moving syllable—
green insects of youth at the intersection
of harvest and time and when the amphora
to the brim filled with must and decades
can no more accept the archaic the bliss
of breath the lantern you held to the world
a show of bravado and genuine trepidation
as verses using your own words tumbled
forth in an unchanging epic of what can never
be completed the separated vowel the clinging
consonant devoted in its nakedness to the goddess
you overwhelmed by red and its multiple absences
the knee length porphyry skirt and the hobson jobson
idiom mugging with strangers in the hills
where unkempt and drunk you took a siesta
that lasted for years in the ear of a jazz trumpet
and waking or seeming to do so and hands full
of letters designations fol-de-rol vomiting
on the sidewalks of your favorite cities *O Poet!*
you yelled into the grimoire where syllables
are deconstructed in the violent saliva of divinity
just who you *were* and *are* and what dumbfounded
gilded tombs erected in your wake and the fellow
travelers in song who one by one fell by the way
why didn't you notice ? the world the evergreen
the symbolic the overdose the strumpet the bright
the catastrophic the child and whatever else
defines your half-second of lamplight
scuttled and tossed aside for your dereliction
inverted pyramids circles and cones and vases
ashes of nameless Mexican cousins topographies
of mountain and oracle seas drained of their lunacy
and the verbiage of hair and perfumes tottering
on the rim of the cosmos green and adolescent
in delivery of totem head-gear the enormous
and final pronoun of the augur it fails here
the birds of reason have long flown and snows
the shop-windows of memory the home-coming
queens in their debacle of ice-cream and nylons
if only you had pertained to the center
fixed your inner eye on the evanescent universe
the hold between your hands the launching
of the perverse hexameter the teachings and babble
of salvation and its bankrupt antiquities
what was it you accomplished ?
alone with the leaf of darkening alone with grief
solitude of the forgotten dialect remorse for all
the wayward mind in its inhibitions gave you
a finger a touch a brother an evening
when grass and its shadow image fade
leaning into the wind that has no origins
in the epoch before time began
the stone   10-15-20

THE ISOLATED ECHO

futile life of the gods
fake disorder of Chaos
one by one the syllables discount
wounds that suffer clouds
proud disdain and fluted doubts
the hundred voids of space
asleep in thunder's absent voice
loud within the metered sepulcher
of poetry the sanctioned rope
never to be rewound
vanishing in hills of vacant color
light takes off its shoes in
cathedrals of grief-stricken shoulders
dawn's bleeding glass horizons
sun that exists below the sea
with bones of lack and fear
heavens without backside
heat with its thousand syllables
records the death of time
lachrymose tables of distance
mirrors of ampersands and
wigs and bodices of Demeter
harvesting dense mountain seasons
calvaries of insects like dust
in swarms of ocher daffodils
how long this goes on without you
what gives the remote its sad fade
who questions the divided god
who dwells in the haunted mouth
what elephants and tortoises
what spear-heads and poisoned fruit
mathematics of the homophone
and fireflies of deduction
the human mind separate
into a dozen hemispheres
we're gone it cries
in tangled sheets of dream
choirs of insane bees
air itself multiplied by two
the archaic fire-stone
altar of burning grass
alas the loss its leaf of tears
darkening in the cell
sign and morph of destiny
your death foregone
in ashen canyons
your death the
isolated echo

10-16-20

PLATO

body of unpronounced syllables !
noun and metronome of the unnamed sky !
useless disorientations of the augurs !
so much in collision with itself
the ego of discounted consonants
the meter of human birth and destruction
recorded in the zig-zag of tortured marble
the quicklime of the mind alive for an instant
before returning to the bitter ash of resolve
the how many and uncounted deaths
on the tip of a finger or in *italics*
the slip of the thumb or the listless eyeball
caught in a communist lunation of thought
caustic immobility of sound–waves
weaving through immolated bricks of envy
gardens of obfuscated greenery the caterpillars
of dawn sawing their way through light
what is to be done about the lingering phoneme
of doubt the transformation of India ?
many the hundreds of voluble spaces
the vaulted dome where ether repeats itself
shores of flame and an entire Asia of ants
is it because air is a multiple of zero
or is it because language has no meaning ?
so much human in the pared fingernail
the isolation ward of missing pages
the circular hemispheres of the number Three
ideas ! if one could only sleep without them
the inevitable resonance of the termite
or water excavated from the wave
what is so mystical about the unshaped hand ?
aloud the fingers sing the eternity of grass
it is a childhood among twins that mirrors
the human condition the agency of depth
the mounting mollusks of fear the *end !*
it is finally the leaf in its inconstancy
of sorrow the limitless darkening
the limitless darkening

10-16-20

WHAT HAS TO BE SAID CANNOT BE PRONOUNCED

the unfinished insect of time has devoured
most the pages of this book leaving little left to say
but the fields and folds of heat lost summers old
have of youth the face dissolved and language
a disorder of conjunctions and ampersands
the volatile drought of airs conjugated senselessly
in the isolation wards of the oracle the enigmas
flashed in their tooth the shining instant
when the body dived into the thumb-sized pool
emerald liquid and wafer-thin waters
what could consciousness assume in the dry-out
the unsheltered thought of music and highways
miraculous neon of intoxication bravura
and epitome of the unspoken vowel
chicanery of the poet using both knees in oratorio
to the gods counted and uncounted who fill
the noon-time horse with the lather of inspiration
won't you be mine it asks constantly on the lawn
where Romeo splits the uneven hemispheres of love
into thirds a knife of mind he recollects
shadows of hands filigree of tempests lightning
that nestles in the leaves of invisible trees
nothing is ever rightly said the mouth has a
proportion of divinity it cannot recognize
until it becomes the disease itself that eats the brain
the famous and fuming disregard for light
a painting of wind splattered with hail-stones
storms of consonants porphyry and heroin
the singing that is vast and inaudible the tombstone
itself the marker that divides the idea
from its circularity and the so many divisions
of the death south of south the land beyond
where there is never a possibility for memory
and the dead themselves crowding the *zócalo*
for the recitation of the months they have abandoned
life ! the prime number the breath of reunion
the smallest and vaguest leaf trembling
on the tip of the branch of night

10-17-20

ANOTHER ORPHIC

"Poeta: jardinero de epitafios"
            Octavio Paz

what's countable about space ?
the number of times I've loved you
went out to the fields of dawn iridescent
each leaf with the face of mourning
both a source and a grave of memory
thinking why am I while X Y and Z
the crepuscular and waning mind as it
slowly disintegrates unable to enumerate
what is infinite and what is immortal
stuttering gods of wind and air
palaces of pleasure glassy erogenous
the fragility of breath and stillness
what gives in the enormous fracture of sky
is the instability of clouds

10-17-20

THE PETRIFIED NOON

twice the sudden fraction that gives life to stone
the imminent sky-storm insufferable madness
to bring havoc to the human tongue and plying
threads of make-believe the illustrious sisters
whose looms weave shrouds of sleeping light
and the shudder and ogives at the top of the stairs
glyphs and clones of cuneiform letterhead
fixtures of density and revolution why don't they
get it straight the polity of inverse proportion
and grass and weed and blowing tarmac and sheets
of unpunctuated text driven by the maenads of
the western hills poignant and grief-stricken
mourners of the feminine plural and diameters
of air with the mathematic intent to reduce mind
to parameters of unspoken language syllabic
unable to comprehend the codifying silences
between statue and statue the great and enormous
finger of memory severed at the tip and whole
columns of cylindrical thought turned vitreous
shuddering in mid air waiting for noon to
petrify the horses of invisibility furious
swart chargers of cloud-semination and trees
wounded and strewn on the edge of a sacred map
waters wastelands and mountains that stagger
like hours of months nameless and rubicund like
fissures in the ether that circles the blackened sun
stationary for days now in its pinnacle of cocktails
dovetailed and concupiscent like charged gods

zoom and cataract and phonetic decay vowels and
asterisks that divide the hemisphere of meaning
from the greater hemisphere of sound rushing
polyphony of augurs divining catastrophes of red
or the unseen quicksilver of the assassins
isn't it enough to have sacrificed the innocent ?
what remains but to inscribe the silenced leaf's
diminutive planets on this incomplete stone ?

10-19-20

LAS AZOTEAS DE TENOCHTITLÁN

half way through time in the center of space
all directions go from the meridian straight north
avoiding south where the dead thrive on monosyllables
and the third hemisphere of time is shortened
by the inch of light it takes to cross sleep's boundaries
mortals puzzle over birth and etymologies
the eye's memories are a confused reticulation
a brief phase in eternity's unfinished ant-hill
dark labyrinth of coagulated stars and waters
spectral resonance of the incomplete noon of marble
when nothing moves but an incremental shimmer
glare and intimation of a sun too soon blackened
by coruscating elements of an aggravated city
traffic of bacchants and hieroglyphs totem Spaniards
who have left behind Galatea and her phantom shepherds
for the colossal gold bricks and unstemmed tide of silver
for the canals of sacred sewage Aztec immolated stone
the top and pinnacle of a single multicolored plume
signaling the end to the first day of a tropical infinity
bulwark of crescent shaped frogs hidden in San Ángel
the possibility that a new year might begin at last
frame of water shivering Toltec vowels embossed
in a mental armor the blaze and rutilation of horses
climbing bone masses and the bruited nonsense
of cadavers by the thousands left to be counted
by augurs who imitate almanacs and friezes
depicting enormous Revolutionary symphonies memory
of children left to dry on rooftops with bleached linens
sacrosanct rags panoply of rust and sugar skulls deaths
by the hundreds with tiny horns blowing hats and wings
terrific parades of cinematic automobiles Dolores del Rio
the saint who ate the pyramids the offal of transgression
mimics and sinners liars at the wheel Porfirio Díaz fading
in the photograph of the Volcano and its slattern wives
gesture of a phonetic *pistolero* to gain his daily share
bread divided into fractions of oxygen and kneeless penitents
of Guanajuato looking for the Surgeon of Nayarit
who will soon be knocking at the door flummoxed and

insensate with pulque the famous red margin of the Hours
draping the pharmacy windows and the blow-out of night
furious and intellectual the dialectic of darkness
smoke and unending neologisms about the Life eternal
to be sought somewhere in El Norte fiction of Hollywood
countless abandoned motors and skins the *frontera*
where the scales of justice tilt gagging on days-old urine
cycles of pathos and iceberg lettuce spine chilling
dreams recollecting the *azoteas* de Tenochtitlán
Chabela and her amazing ink-spent hair the wind
that takes its ropes and ties them around the Cathedral
lifting from earth the archaic architecture of oblivion
while worms with the mistaken eyes of devastated gods
who live on cigarettes and cerveza in cantinas
of peeling wallpaper and fly-swatters create words
circular and soundless echoes tinny subtractions
discarded illegible typescript on onion skin *History*

10-19-20

THE SONG OF TWINS

I am double the twice of grass
twin of a thousand ruined afternoons
heat in the form of a bee's wing
plantation of shade and echo
vision of the over-burdened plum tree
brother to the gravel of the driveway
bicycle and wheel-barrow in the garage
long-rimmed glasses worn for the first time
in order to see the dark inside the sun
I am whatever is leftover of sound
when it has exhausted the noontime air
how bright the consequence of living
lying on my back next to him
what is other than a more of less
the whim of delicate shapes coming
forth from the elixir of time
to guess that what is round
is memory and its phonetic variations
that what is a hill is removable
that the street behind the empty lot
is where they dug for bones
the remains of sleep inside one's double
antiquities in a willow leaf
whistling so loud none can hear
the phantom dog we consecrated
in the nearest river we could find
I am I guess my brother's hidden half
evening transcending its own vibration

a sky half full with unseen angels
the airplane manned by a dead uncle
zooming in the ear of the other side
what ho Brother the loss is here
continents of clouds and gravity
worlds tumbled from a kite
or smaller still the empty hour
asleep with you I don't know where

10-19-20

FIAT LUX

all that matters is light aphasic and lunatic
light that lacks direction and gravity light
architecture of the eye memorizing light
mind ignited by madness of light a blaze !
the insomnia of light the enormous fictions
of space-travel on beams of light the caustic
reveries and deifications of light its cities
by the banks of non-existent rivers and
its lovers holding hands of shadow-play
orients of light with its weightless mountains
goddesses of light with waists of invisible honey
hair of light fantastic arrays where planets nest
suns of black light ultra-violet homophones
and the descant of light mythic deformations
called fire and ether and supple nouns
that burn all night and eyes with monsoons
of light discharges of lunar radiance rains
pouring from clouds of mysteriously unseen
light and batteries and torches and pyres
the dead who are the extinction of light
whose voices echo through canyons of ears
mourning the loss of light the lessened glow
lamps and fireflies and screens where light
dances with memories of bright and shining
light the everlasting which was created just
yesterday in a crevice of space by accident
or design the furiously voyaging sheaves of light
fields where light is harvested and evenings
when sorrow and sunset complaint and grief
consume the darkening leaves whose small
voices are the inaudible vowels of light

10-20-20

OCTOBER ORPHIC SONNET

talking about this and that floods cities
ancient and crepuscular the densities marked
by eyelashes of blood hematite and brick the
streets slick that are sources of rain and
sweetness by dawn's aerial statues neighing
brightly and hoses aimed at the sleep of many
dreamed it was only yesterday history of rock-
fragments formations of light by molecular
hands the gravity of ether falling into trance
or just once if never the accident of love
delicacy shared on the fifth floor where
no elevator reaches secret symposium of
a sudden grief too the all consuming throb
remembering the swept and yellow echo

10-20-20

IS BUDDHA A NOUN OR AN IMPERATIVE ?

Wake up ! empty it out ! Wake up !
the numinous void that runs through all names
the things that lack qualities the weights
and measures the eye filters in draughts
distances and rumors of light and bees
grown hoarse with warning the air made heavy
in its seventy varieties and x-rays of ultra-violet
and shades that narrow the definition of sight
naked mountains sutras rice-wine hell
sitting just sitting until *Bong* the clangors
of human noise and nerve rutilations of
emotion the confused passions and desires
of being the very oceans of sin and virtue
Pfah ! skeleton of light bereft of sinew and
meaning nothing but sound the famous
unheard Note the fantasies of seers to *know*
they are all women even in their virility
the professed singers and bards nothing
but clouds the envy of blank registers
mantras going ding-dong until the hours
turn to wax melting in the charged
noon of eternity and edges that don't hold
and photographs of the center of space
birds lifted like wind-up toys in the small
heaven of the wall and then when it's all up
and the shouting and din are impalpable
dust in the ear that has been surrendered
to *Shah Jehan* and marble entities swarm
the altar piece where the nuptial vows Burn
what is to wake but vowels and incense

smoking lantern the mind !
I am not the creator / I do not move

10-21-20

DEATH STOOD ON ONE FOOT
FOR TWENTY MILLION YEARS

she was just a girl with red ribbons
in her hair and no obligations despite
what she had been told to do and holding
her breath and withstanding the violence
of air and the atoms that submerge night
for several eternities herself was changeless
the immobility of the world of light in
her eye became the lightning blitz
that repeatedly destroys Shiva's creation
on one foot and not the other then tiring
of either foot repaired to Mount Meru
and became as a log unconscious in
the infinite sleep of ants or fire-flies
and dreamed she was a mannequin
behind plate glass windows a show-off
a thing of glitz and cinema a reckless
waif born to be wild driving cars off
cliffs for a living maddening with her
looks whoever met her into despair and
insanity every mortal sooner dead than
breathe another day of light and so it was
she fulfilled her obligation even asleep
a trunk of dead-wood atop Mount Meru

10-21-20

THREE OCTOBER SONNETS

steep ascent the heart's night trek
dazzle spent stars into crushed organdy
plunge and thoughts amiss and rains
with their forty hour spells the mind numbs
hastening to its dumb daily morgue
are Thursdays any better since the last
has passed and numinous light-storms
a flicker in the sky's lost backyard
leaves gather their own sound-track
rushing wildly in the gutters of memory
a sweet friend a phantom a counterpart
the girl in pinafore frock her kempt
design the sandy mausoleum fading
pattern of sleep's circular silence

the text is the body and letters a sign
a missive from beyond the soul a form
without shape not pronounced a vowel
of smoke an absence of consonants a
syllable misinformed and repeated to
no avail the memory of noise the ear
retains and sleeping distances and
repercussions the world of the bee
wayward wings too swift to see and
light in response to gravity shifts
from its dark birth into the shelter
of rustling leaves the house and wall
of dreams none can apprehend the small
cursive hand and the polished nail

language you may remark is the darkness
spoken not in leaves but in some wayward
past a loss of signatures a flurry and buzz
somewhere in the air or the incognito
simply of pronouns words you cannot say
without rightly falling from the abstract
into the pilings gathered below water
the doom-spell of dreams a wavering anti-
light of sounds distinctions erased curving
around the nocturnal absence a frame
shot through with longing and vowels
misplaced like stars lost from view
you will pause and lingering realize
the reflection in the glass is not yours

10-22-20

DEBATE BETWEEN POLITICIAN AND MOUNTEBANK

the idiom at the end of the tunnel supported
by runaway syllables of the chastised gods
who lost their heads in a row with language
now it all comes down to not just loss of identity
but the race of mortals the waffling wobbling
planet the darkness and evil that are intent
and dialect after dialect surrendered to arms
the race for a weaponry that will strike at
the heart of the cosmos and destroy it leaving
what was shining an instant of alabaster
statuary honoring the myth of human speech
but why go on the tender condition of skin
and bones the contrition of the ventilator
or the surgeon coping with the direction of
thought maimed and wayward the beauties
once glimpsed between cycles of mountains
the unabashed horizon stripped of its distance
who wins the race is sooner dead and lifeless
even as the laurel leaves that wither about
the temples abandon their whisper of color
green and sympathy and innocence

10-23-20

SELF AWARENESS

don't want to be anymore the person that I am
no longer remain with the name that *identifies* I me
burden of memory that stays in the same head
is most of the time the other reality the senseless
alien who has stolen my shadow the I me was who
then when why and what was that I me questions
suffix and prefix sound and lack brief and length
hours when sun stands still was brother me I then
what park and stone tree and weed shade and
glint glass and brick reality confounds reality
walking incessantly home divergent truths a
whim a quirk of fate a street that is sudden and
lore of books always with newer words and pictures
glyphs and cuts and inserts and maps an index
without alphabet like the Greeks for the first time
has will and swings or seesaws evenings surprise
eye takes it back hiding pronouns in cellars
reeking dandelion wine and urine someone there
mindless to frighten the soul out if its shell and
sacred or scared that moment me I who fell
away from the faint and sidewise a stepping
into rock formations or a stream of afternoons
staring eternity in the face blinking until savage

solar noises and everything as before birth I
never was

10-23-20

ARGONAUTS

the sacrificial ridge the looms and waves that
dark and purplish run the stiff horizon to its end
was ever thus the punctuations of needless fate
young and reckless the unheeding youth bent
to steer the skiff to its burning goal and cheer high
the fainting day the glory of the blotted sun the black
and ominous the bleak that hovers like a mountain
in the sweep of chilling sleep did ever the voices
learn to ring sound and right in display of humanity
or is the echo all that stirs in the heart's coruscated
valves the chance of memory in its narrow syllable
that flattened noise of catastrophe in dreams that
never begin and through volleys of blazing vowels
and consonants that lose all weight what's to speak
how to say the junctions of stars and grasses have
no purpose in the map that lacks center in a fury
of space and boundless emptiness a fraction was
the force of light the fierce few seconds of play
in summer fields the enigmatic and tossed phrases
like hands of wind or blossoms of unseen air so why
return to formless rock to caverns of nocturnal sorrow
grief between the knees and harsher yet that burdens
mortal shoulders and astray the feet that lead here
and there to ruins of leaf and repercussions green
small ears and lesser yet the final diapason of breath

10-24-20

POEM IN THE SHAPE OF AN INVISIBLE VOLCANO
para mis amigos de Somos en Escrito

lava flowers colored like evening's red and gold
cities crescent-shaped and buried in a trance of cinders
elevated ruins of the only remaining statue of Persephone
elegance of hands cut from their pulse and shadowless
Moorish architecture of the eyebrows of Vanity
symbolism and margin of all phonetic errors
power of silent detonations deep within the heart
and clamoring for meat of the soul those denied passion
stars divided in half at the molten strike of noon
rhapsodies of words that have more sound than meaning
the shapeless intuition of light to transcend itself
in a glorious burst of sunflowers and solar homophones
the tryst of lunatic and aphasic in the sewers of Tenochtitlán
rain in porphyry torrents pouring from a cloudless sky
and mortals like blind birds circling their own destruction
with the tiny feet of a lost poetic meter and bewailing
the day when thunder and mountain joined forces
men who believed the sea was only a hemisphere of sleep
and waves always feminine and plural were at the root
of the enigma caused by consciousness at birth
etymologies of distance and repercussion like drum-rolls
in the faint ear of the adolescent afternoon assassin
was love ever more futile and gorgeous in its escape ?
sentient ovals of the moon in its perpetual fade
aspirin and silken ropes that tie the shadow down
to a body that has only existed in pharaonic dreams
the constant disrepair of language
illiteracy of the gramophone and sewing machine
the enormous and inexplicable circularities of heat
coupled with the mysterious rumors of mummies
grief ! legends of the half-formed antiquities of rock
tragic association of the sorrowing trigger finger
and the dizzying instamatic nature of fire-flies
death over and over in small print at the bottom
and pages of water and fluid discrepancies of thought
rushing in all directions with nowhere to go
skies decrepit with the gods of mistaken pronouns
oracle and augury and spit-fire demons wayward desires
the entire panoply of historic deviation
one by one the children and the dead going south
volumes of unused scripts the crying at the end
the sadness of leaves bereft of their own speech
the longing and drift of undetected planets
asleep forever between eons of galactic despair

10-25-20

TWO UNTRANSLATED SONNETS

learning to write by rote letters of air
pure memory the silent syllables that echo
deafening the tympanum with speech of
the gods in their incessant drum-roll of distance
the repercussion of empty hours of leaves
about to abandon their own darkness
becoming as outlines of light in the tumult
when were we ever sure of our own speech
the one hand that writes the other that erases
doubled by doubt anxiety produces mind
and mind waking signals to itself a mirror
image of someone left far behind in time
the other the useless shadow-form following
the voice of stars long since gone to sleep

the familiar is what is lost in grasses
where abandoned hands sleep with memories
of flight and clouds of absence and depth
roads winding around the self-same stone
a hill with arrows pointing to the trees
that surrender their capacities to night
leaves and human thought darkening
together in the small knot of light that
ties previous lives to this fading being
questions in the shapes of rock and sand
eerie distances where feet have yet to step
children wrapped like mummies in kites
let loose in the eternities of a single afternoon
skies that rain enigmas of pure sound

10-26-20

FOR EURYDICE AN UNHEARD SONG

shepherd who were you in the vast and ancient corn-fields
beneath what withering blackened sun of fruitless heat
was to wander your gambit love-fooled from motel to
labyrinthine motel in cities turned archaic in an instant
poppies roses hyacinth and chrysanthemums bedecked
the beloved's hair the traipsing nymph through waters
distant and glistening with repercussions of the sky
around the secret planets that last for but a day
libraries opened symphonies of unwritten pages clouds
of syllables no ear can withstand troubadours singing
in decibels sustained by bee-swarms in the yellow chaos
of an eternal afternoon when backwards or front
the oaths of music and mystical reunion dazzled like
the metallic signatures of the gods who live on smoke
and regeneration and what applause was that thundering
in the promise to never see again yet in flight heights
obtained in daedalian contradictions of air and space
alert you were to almost nothing numbed by the savage
inwit of love's perpetual and instantaneous oblivion
what shepherd were you amongst the blackberry and
the living thorn the crescent greenery of a missing spring
the small waters that make sleep seem greater than it is
what confounded realties in the ear of wheat or the ballad
of mown grass the romance of mistaken sunsets the eons
in a hidden vowel that rhymes with the end of time
come back ! it all flees down the wrong way street
the horses of the rented solar disk or the heroic verses
of a perfect but incomplete adolescence – shepherd !
you were alive you ran and stumbled you gestured to
infinity and the manacled constellations of an inverted
heaven where angels of spark and burning wing change
hands only to descend and partake of your pale grief
earthling wounded by the invisible alphabet of desire
leaf and sorrow evenings in the darkness of the hill
no language of glyph and sound will bring *her* back
echoes and only echoes that linger in the rock
echoes and echoes only that vanish in the heat

10-27-20

A BOUQUET FOR MY WIFE
58th wedding anniversary

can the second or third choruses of the hymn divine
or the vowels of intricate concord of the unheard song
rival in any way the golden budding chrysanthemums
of our multiple autumn dream the furious passing
season of streams and repercussions of distance
and the clouds of a framework that defines love
not as the instant play of sound and mind but
the eternal symptom of reunions in the afterthought
that unites at first sight the memory of junctions
of ether and legendary rock too high above or
too far below the ordinary phrase of swarming bees
alive together the threads that bind and petals swooning
in the untenanted air of ideals that cannot apply
to the fervent and maddened moment of our harmony

10-27-20

SHE WHO IS THE SHAPE OF NIGHT

impeccably dressed in bark and waist held
together by darkening ivy *Parvati*
at play with dice and astronomy promises
with the touch of her teeth to love forever
the nostalgia of skin the pearled beads
that run down from her temples the single
finger of the number *fivethousandandfive*
with which she whittles time down to its
only inch how divine the crescent rising
in each eye the leveled beam of light that
destroys what she desires the man inside
the thigh quivering with sacred lust
and all memory of the god who devoured
her in dreams of water and endless sound
great repercussion of thought mind struggling
to breathe breasts poised to remain static
in the event of cosmic annihilation
how many and often the eons of an afternoon
when the phantom in antelope skin races
the highway to its catastrophic end
and wheels that have no start or finish
keep running their ampersands over
all trace of mortal vanity and poets
pinned to golden clouds try to efface
the outlines of her unpronounced consonants
nocturnal constellations and black holes
she maintains in the aphasia of her intimacy
Parvati ! the chiseled obverse of the royal coin
hair of a million inks and kalpas of reunion

and denigration the most beautiful orient
disguised in the plenitude of the void
as the girl thirteen years of age
who high on *Bang* and *Ganja* entered
the temple of heated Penance devoting
herself to the Unfinished Left-handed god
in whom she dissolved a shift of yellow pollen
eyelids and salvations of revolving planets
houses of phonetic decay labyrinths
of repeated eternities without sequence
she who is the shape of night
letter of the broken elephantine tusk
wound and cicatrix of the shattered air
indestructible mountain of irreversible orgasm
heights and depths of Nowhere !
in longing there is no before or after
only the thin residue of a vermilion powder
fire burned by fire
nostalgia

10-28-20

THE SYMPOSIUM

"Oímos por espejos"
Lorca

this afternoon we discuss the state of poetry
the archaic oriental ancient unfinished rock formation
cliffs of rumor compacted into a few variable sounds
the one you left behind in sleep is greater for
its absence and the one you keep repeating as
you stutter is the divine syllable not meant for human
mirrors the ear and its occidental other stilled
by a single blade of grass symbol of darkening
and grief and as you pause for a moment sitting there
discussing the state and condition of the already ruined
art of the *incomplete* you have second thoughts
it didn't come from Ionia it wasn't even in existence
when they came over the Hindu Kush maybe it's
not polite to maintain this symposium and the others
ragged hermaphrodites with bodies borrowed from
some pre-Christian novel you oppose the direction
their loosened vowels are taking projecting solemn auguries
about the flight of skies about the inverted afternoons of Hades
the Stygian helmsman and his broken oars the overloaded
verses of tempest and bird-wing the adorned and adorable
dead putti the fringes of sound the mind in its vocabulary
of hesitation and phonetic spectra how is one to sleep
with a head full of abracadabra and nonsensical whims
about the origins of the Muses mountain born and
dressed like kites or quicksilver inspirations to song

and dance the nodding epithets and glories whatever
the discussion is not straightforward drunken tousle-haired
young men with skins of antelope or leopard how graceful
their presences which just as soon disintegrate and the volume
turned way up and cigarette chatter and gods of the sudden
entrance appearing and disappearing clatter junk and
long draughts of mescal and what can you do your fingers
isolated from the rhymes and meters and a host
of Latin pejoratives and dialect of rumor and repercussion
the sea comes up to your knees and sunsets of Spanish gold
and the vitriol of lovers who envy and nothing more
what is there to explain and the anthologies spill open
flower-fields and names like Eurydice or Beatrice
abound and you look over your shoulder at Night
secretive and whispering into a bottle that holds
the Sybil green and upside down vatic maniac tongue
that none can understand the very bedlam and manicomio
that poetry *should* be you try to assert but for
the nymphs holding up drowned Hylas and the rivers
rushing to lose identity and name and the Chaos
of all human endeavor the critics and circus-masters
naysayers and idolaters the fashion-worshippers
and finally tiny and redundant in appearance the Rishis
naked and dazed smeared with Vedic mantras uttering
and stammering with their knees the ultimate truths
the One and the Many and the Goddess the shimmer
of distance and Echo her manifold faces and hair
but for a moment visible before all the smoke and ashes
and Memory disappear and left alone in an Empty Room
you with the ghosts of Longing and Leaf
Silencio !

10-28-20

THE MYTH OF ETERNAL RETURN

completed the nine hell-cycles the tenth one
begins with butterflies of shadow leaves of night
chattering jays children in the eaves about
to be re-born as lizards or fluttering white moths
deaths can never be counted a day after the loss of time
the road that can only lead south shrouded by willow
and honeysuckle and the ivy that wraps around mind
turning red at the undefined hour what are they
but asterisks and plunging suffixes in the hazard
of renovation and chaos yet unheard voices still sing
like brief light-strokes on a clock that lacks hands
edges of water and a center dispersed every minute
that passes from the tiny garden-dial to the greater
homophone of the sun turning mysteriously black
in the rush to bury its teeming head in mountains
that bear sleep from the inky vastness of memory
skirts of inverted rose petals envy of the rising star
dawns that first appear in the eyes of horses
drawing the wain of thought across immensities
that span the distance between thumb and index
each passing moment contains the whole of time
grasses and the full weight of unseen clouds
streams reflecting the repercussions of a summer
when wind and heat shape the forgotten vowel
and the ear of deathly language puts itself to slumber
beneath the rock that recounts no tale

10-29-20

THE ABSENT VOICE OF SLEEP
El pasado está inhabitable
Lorca

have come to where days have but one wing
the wind has ceased moving and earth divided
into five unequal hemispheres has forgotten
how to sing but for distances and their echoes
buried in hills of opalescent verdure and beneath
moons tottering on tricycles because pronouns
are seasons of abandoned rumors stammering
that life is an untruth of weeping and walls
are the subjunctive of yesterday as for the future
which began a million years ago today it is dust
a vermilion chaos demanding coherence and justice
for the numeral three the boomerang of counting
when death is imminent and hours of sand and
glass have come to a silence of repercussion and
is it a wonder that the coffin insists on its script
and the color of air is an improbable weight
we have seclusions and eyelids and ears attuned
to the sound night makes turning to rock crystal
stars ! weeds and the invisible sutures of clouds
childhood the minimal bee-sting in sleep and
yellow which is devastation and secrets hidden
in the leaf whose infinite memory is loss of water
why ! the house by the roadside is an abyss a formula
of doors and pyramids and small brick Tuesdays
when the body is laid out as a floral pattern and *yes*
the hues of thought the conjunction of mirror and
asterisk the notorious moment of the window
which is the endless hiatus between dreams and
lawns and slopes and iridescent cliffs hurtling
like a poem into the aphasia of grief and mourning
grasses darkened in an imponderable chloroform

10-30-20

RING OF FIRE

loosely designed in envelops of muslin and silk
the devotionals begin with matins at the stroke
of fire in triplicate entrance of Dawn ushered
with her horses five the igneous and evocative who
hoofed and saddled all gold and edge the confines
break all space opens up double of what it was
last night and speaking through an egress of vowels
the hemisphere that belongs to doors shifts its
weight and Lo the spectacle of light the portion
of life that seems so fragile are you with me ?
comes down and stands at the lintel the bravery
of hair and ink her face a rotundity of distance
why doesn't she and who is the pronoun at her
elbow wanting and aching to know the levels
of comprehension and language even as stirring
grass darkens to the right of the worlds that
plunge through sleep's unfelt surface evidence
that nothing can happen and the silences of
drum and mantel and the furious equivalence
of time with its twin *death* suffice before roseate
echoes of an unburdened sea the probability of
day the shape of gravity in its perilous descent
from the origins and twice again the ignition flares
mind's earliest thought to bare armed Psyche turns
embraced for hours without end and what's more
the hurry of grass the back and forth of leaves
rock and stone climbing higher and the depths
that reveal the *other* goddess of the Unknown
great seeming day-lamp ! bright poetry !
through countless windows the fire!
one day I will enter the circle and
touch that *fire*

10-31-20

POST MORTEM
> *La mar no tiene naranjas*
> Lorca

how did I see it the day I died
if not as one born in a town
whose population was thirty below zero
lilac spray and hills submerged in skirts
dancing in the moon's small snows
x- rays of other lives and clinics
for those who cannot drive
how to reach the next municipality
if roads remain unmapped ?
distances and echoes of trees
or arroyos excavated of their weeds
when summer stopped beneath the bell
and sounded its own death knell
sequences of heat and pools lifted
by levers to a denied heaven
in and amongst them I surrendered
my twin's oblique green shadow
under lids of hematite and ivory
lesser worlds swarmed like blind bees
the fossil estuary where I lay my head
the rushing grasses of unknown fields
places where I stepped and fell from time
are the cliffs of oblivion shorn
from their epic & tempestuous seas ?
Latin curses and homonyms for wind
suns blackened by an Aztec cipher
enigma of the separated vowel
endgame of the Carretera Panamericana
poetry constantly incomplete
verses of leaf stone and eglantine
troubadour of the unconscious eye
stoned on the solar consonant
to have failed algebra and geometry
condemned to a Moroccan medina
wandering in Dante's labyrinth
what an error to have survived
the extra hour of Persephone's
dismissal face down in humus
detritus of chaotic memory
the day I died the pantomime
'pon *thy* gilded tomb dumfounded
in ethereal silence

11-01-20

DÍA DE LOS MUERTOS
Max and his uncle Joe

death's many signatures in Sicily's quicksilver seas
the moon and its argent micronauts
uncounted in the recesses of Sierra Madre
actors with faces of timeless burros
named Cárdenas foraging in sugar cane
coldness at the center of the sun
seventeen years or forty nine years
the instant is the same for whatever happens
the body is only the *thought* of the body
incense and wharves of the conquistadores
liana and ivy snares at the hour's *second* end
how often this occurs and cannot recall
the why and which the who and wherefore
the canals of Tenochtitlán lose their way
among withered rooftop garlands
I remember *nothing* after pushing the green button
but salutes of armless angels the rose
through which a river pours and summers that
belong to memory's only syllable and heat
the roar of Aetna's ovens twenty marigold flowers
Narcissus and Hyacinth eye and pulp of
repercussion blindness of water and depths
where night's riddle threads an unheard harp
calacas y calaveras ! thousands at play
with missing fingers nameless deities
in a single afternoon making rosaries of light
smoke snaking through vowels of perpetuity
toys that imitate sleep's small noises
tender the hair that falls around the wing
shimmering hues of nacre consonants
why is speech so difficult today ?
colibrí ! ruby-throated messenger of death
clouds the size of silence and glass
motion and gravity have lost all sense
evening fades in the vestibule of echo
one hand seeks the other
in an abyss of shape
darkness of words
dos mariposas de la noche !

11-01-20

THE UNINTENDED SYLLABLE OF MEMORY

what is a document map ? is it spellbound ?
the charge is in red today the ovations are
voiced in silence the flitting curtains at the windows
are spirits plaintively looking for the thoughts
they left behind when they occupied bodies
lawns are inhabited by houses long empty
and the horses of dawn with their nitrous flares
and brooding patient muscles plunge to the hills
where we used to play a lyric a flower a stone
and hard by the shade grove the rustling stream
was hell that near ? can still hear the bee swarms
bring an end to July for the last time and the sky
reddening with coruscations of the great texts
scholiasts and footnotes about love ! Venus ?
futility of marble and the intent of speech
lengthy pages in fading glyphs and Persians
and Chinese vying for empire of all things
on this day when with spikenard and essence
of distilled waters perfumes that gods employ
weeping we recall the spirits at the window curtains
and sheets and the attics where airplanes hang
from invisible threads and the wars and battles
and all that vague patriotic nonsense dust and smoke
when we can only score some notches in the air
twilight and the enormous chorus of crickets
memory's long unintended syllable
before night returns with its damaged songs
stellar disorientations muses caught off guard
light separated from its shadow
leaves the darkness of their voices

11-02-20

ON THE EVE OF THE ELECTION 2020

in the clearing the Ojibway sing their song
and by the marsh Hiawatha stands watching
the red eyed deer disappear in the stolen west
woodpecker mallard and haunting loon
birch bark and willow and lost afternoon
the world as it seems is an instant too brief
light and the vagaries of cloud and thunder
and months that have been without count
the dead especially who drape drumheads
with mists of mourning and circle left to
right near an asphalt strip that leads nowhere
a bus that carries three dozen school kids
comes and goes past blinking lamps and
signs effaced by time and the skies above
with envelopes of tempest and dark lakes
sun itself tarnishes with its cold dreams
of a missing orient the cycles of cosmic
generation and the multiple heads of buffalo
who have no water left to drink and thoughts
and stellar homophones that appear at noon
surprise the wooden statue of the godhead
the burning that turns living bone to ash
the ridge of conifers trembles like an eye
of disbelief blinded by small cinder-showers
that mantle the suburb with an early night
what else gives weight to the polluted air
abundance of oil-slicks like glistening ponds
hanging in mid-air and ask you then are
these the precincts peopled by lowly humans
hunters and predators of the uncast vote
bars remain open 36 hours a day where
offspring of European kingdoms drink
their swill and raise chants of loud victory
to the Great-White-Father the lurching
demon wearing purloined antlers and
automatic rifle by his side and riot squads
and trashed containers of canned heat
curse of minions the abrupt end of time
dwindling bushes and arcades of foliage
once verdant rust colored in hues of hate
++++++++++++++++++++++++++++++++
Ojibway and Lakota nations shadow-dance
in schools of abandoned books and whisper
cries filling creek and arroyo with sadness
magenta tinted the moon rises enormous
above rock formations and vacancies of earth
tilled furrows where calendars of corn
once grew a November wasteland now
broken arrows buried deep in echoes
that no memory can revive

11-02-20

CANCIÓN DE NOVIEMBRE

do we ever remember who we are ?
time to pass to the other hemisphere
the dream of the body and what it contains
anxiety of statues doves without wings
skies the size of a dime rushing into flame
the absence of names rumors of upland grasses
figures of speech clouds and mists without vowels
the diadem of darkness that fits over the brow
the chaste Diana with murder in her eyes
do we ever remember who we are ?

11-03-20

SCHICKSALSLIED

the world belongs to the dead
the circulation of thoughts always tends
to the south where the innumerable ones
gather in their hundred-door quarters
dividing and multiplying and subtracting
the meters that compose every mortal
vein and leaf sound and stillness
rock and the empire of ants and darkness
the center is nowhere echo emanates from nowhere
skies are nacre plates encrusted with planets
immobile and dusty and stars have no passion
frozen eminences just inches above the head
mind is flush with streams that go haywire
looking for the subterranean passage
what are bees but vocabulary lists gone wild ?
the world belongs to the dead
and yet we claim possession of this or that fief
memory is a sieve of night and fireflies
bodies are what we dream and faces
the opposition of mirrors and waters
everywhere is south the great Dravidian fraction
of dialect and phonetic decay and ears
drilled with attempts at meaning
vowels shattered at their inception lingo
and shunt imitations of the speech of the gods
babble and stutter aphasia the dead talking
in their endless sleep emitting consonants
rotund and ruddy which we try to apprehend
waking is a nomad's curse stalking realms
without paths and directions just the looming
impassivity of distance and gravity
dare we ? belong to the dead lawns and
structures of shadow and ossuaries where
we lay the head memorizing the days of light

allotted to us just minutes ago
continents without calendars and houses
where ruminants with great staring eyes
devour the roots of mountains
there is no delight but in darkness
where fire eats fire

11-03-20

NEPENTHE

Neptune ! where has your guitar gone ?
plangent waters dissected by repercussions
of light lethal and gorgeous breaking over
the Olympian summits a pit and a wasteland
simmering stygian shoals and numbers that
cannot be reckoned like shattered clouds
that cannot be reshaped and what of that
music and the broken strings and plectrum
you once tuned to the ascension of vowels
Neptune ! your instrument of divine resonance
and harmony vanished in deceitful waves
that no longer pound angelic drumheads
nor wearing seal-skin leap the dancers IO!
everything is distance now the unframed
vistas the misted eye the drained ear the
and the and the fierce rock-entities of sleep
dream speech ineluctable syllables liquid
and dense saying things not meant to be heard
oracular and enigmatic as the leaf in the seer's
mouth baleful dark issuing from tongues
of fire ashes and broken finger-nails and
the Grecian bark listing in the morning storm
eddying and rushing streams tides higher than
the blackened sun's swift arc and horses
sacred to Neptune unchecked scattered racing
into aqueous mountain-domain of deadly Nymphs
grotto and sepulcher sinister abode of Hylas
and proud Narcissus *H20* clue to godhead
invisibility of all emotions drowned grasses
Neptune ! your trident has ceased singing !
blood and salt and the ichor of the gods
plasma and make-believe of the human
condition and shoulders sorrowing deep
like *cante jondo* profound and unknown
each knee a garbled prayer for salvation
++++++++++++++++++++++++++++++++
it is day of submersion and irreversible sounds
hours of cities and sand-mounds naked kids
chasing surf backwards into the archaic dark
heat irremediable circling air like a noose

perspiration of goddesses ! conch and nautilus
toys of sparkling mirage and longing
Neptune ! not an iota of you in sight !
arenas of echo and oncoming night
the end of everything meaningful only
the only of grief tangled algae bleached bone
awash by the steep cliffs of *Nepenthe*

11-04-20

THE ABSENT WORD THAT SUSTAINS US

> "Ma Sibilla, che cosa vuoi?"
> "Ma io voglio morire"
>   *Sanguineti/Petronio, Satyricon*

in the grammar book of the winds there is no direction
the least careful of the bees has lost its sight
and flowers unexpectedly wild make a ruin of the path
how frequent have we tried to learn the lesson
but without wings and always forgetting *how*
we lack the letters to spell our thoughts and
in the maze of summer air mistake the hand
for what it shapes and underfoot the dark realms
moan and hummingbirds from the star of death
hover speeding through the bright labyrinth
who of us can name the first Greek who died
beneath the rotating wheels of Love's mad god
nor can aspire to hold the body close of one
who in his own image drowned sweet child alas

dressed in the dark syllables of absence and echo
the dialect that issues from the mouths of leaves
the grassy entwined nouns that make no sense
nor the constant pounding of the solar homophone
in the ears of corn surrendered to tomes of blazing heat
myth of the round shape the circling spheres of sound
a music in the yellow re-formation of bright air
the hands that spiral dizzying in unseen swarms
of bee and dragonfly the very nuance of vowels
pronounced in sleep languid vestiges of breath
what was the call that shuddered in the dust
the fallen acre of tormented sky the failing moons
ellipses of memory small growths of mind and
structures of longing the grief of clouds

was the stream we stepped the flowing hair away
slight of face the unremembered boy the waist
up to the waters of a darkened afternoon and
did single out the flexion of a lost adjective
pronouns of trees the conjugated breezes adorned

the leaves and not require the hand to repair its
shadow the plight of air in mourning absences
no word it was that held us tight in memory's sweet
hive the buzz of distances and hills shaking dusk
the invisible shapes of setting like suns of liquid
gold their ancient haunt of black underground
the foot that never felt nor the brief white
cry of Persephone what tissues spun in the eye
witness the furious and archaic sky's lament

11-05-20

THE BLACK HOLE

who occupies all of space
yet has no inch to fulfill
void of thought supreme
mind the inside out of light
who claims a thousand names
four faces five top-knots and eyes
more than stars that dispel night
sparse zoologies liquid verses
molten consonants houses
in which the Unknown dwells
horses by midday scattered
across the northern half
the south a wasteland burning
smoke the height of sky numinous
vowels dangling like ear-rings
from lobes of celestial nymphs
water was once the reckoning
rushing turbulence of unspoken
words empty as stone underneath
where earth and sea vie in sound
speed of silence unbound and fires
tied to all previous births
paper roses men of one dimension
no future beckons to the present
wild grasses strangle purpose
mirages ruddy as the kine
ruminating on the other side
of space in whose enormous eyes
Dawn shifts a phantom thing
her lamp forever nameless
that brings to dewy mortals
death's useless pronouns
and days brief as insects
darkening in an afternoon

11-06-20

BALLAD OF DEATH IN THE TIME OF COVID

what is once but the other side of twice ?
legends of earth in a single deep furrow
births and loss of memory the verdure
of instantaneous the trill that fills the sky
when was the hand ever its other
or the shadow the body of the soul ?
death casually walks in and out of
taverns packed by noon with hustlers
drunkards cheat a winning ace of spades
and eyelids fall from paintings on the wall
death sits casually on the bar stool
and orders gin and tonic with a slice of lime
I've seen it all before and been here twice again
they insert stolen pages in the book
and claim that Spain was never won
Moors hold all of Africa with a bare scimitar
it's all a rant of false victories declared
death lounges casually deep into the afternoon
a swizzle stick and some andalusian olives
the treasure that glitters in his eyes
the scepter held in his invisible fists
the headlines that proclaim everlasting war
Jihadists wielding black parasols and
translators of the latest holy versions
hand-wrestle for empire on public library steps
death gingerly steps over homeless corpses
and laughs darkly up his sleeves
these cities of salt and concrete drives
and structures higher than a knife –
what are they but dormant ant-heaps
mausoleums of unforgiven bodies foul
I've seen it all before and been here twice again
up and down Fifth Avenue a vacant waste
where automobiles stall and fashion-whores
dismount from horses of digitized renown
and death gracefully moves with his cigarette
a pretty girl slung on either arm through
traffic indivisible and unheard blaring horns
and asks in accents of distant grieving
what is once but the other side of twice ?

11-07-20

A SMALL NOVEMBER SONG

the fifth is next to nothing in despair
sunlight follows hills into archaic depths
and buried with the smallest white a cry
from some mistaken moon a body behind
glass and death in tiny rivulets of silver
brooding chasms of thought night the one
and only spangled with wasted asterisks
and diplomas of planetary loss a wonder
to survive the hour and join longing to its
myth of leaf and bower how distant green
the darkened hand and slighter still the ring
loosened from the finger toiling in the grass
memory slides off the stone and less than
three the ancient mind can only grieve
the unfound day the blackest sun purveys
the drum that touches water in its decay
sounding vowels of mourning and hues
that cloud horizons with drained oblivion

11-07-20

ROMANCE DEL HIJO PERDIDO

suns and moons like burnished hills afar
from a sky of lessened vowels flung into lesions
and arroyos drunk on quicksilver memories
planets half-named for mountains and roses
junkets of light traipsing around stalks of air
idioms and repercussions of shapeless clouds
the earth an inch from Olympus and Olympus
a depth of myth and despair this and that who
follows breath in its labyrinthine formations
a life to give and take away an obscure number
a syllable that cannot be said and the ear a buzz
of hives refrained from sleep in its indigo cage of
dreams longing and some grief borne on backs
of cliffs and *hear* the resonance of a sea behind
the metaphors of solitude this step taken aback
this tale of resin and marigolds this notation of
gravel and similes of smoke an architecture of
azure replicated in ink where letters and ivory
drown submerged like petals in the morning
plucked and left for hummingbirds to drain
how distant like a mother's forlorn asterisk
smoldering grass of loss or disrepair a *child*
mourned in the lily shafts and left to drift alone
on pharaonic waterways leading to serpentines
of musk and nascent lotus streams of oblivion
this romance of dialects and troubadours aphasia

and phonetic dissonance haunting of a lunar
stone transfixed by briar and hyacinth yesterday
who knew the only way was the one that goes
through flame ? ash and cinders underfoot
the dismantled shadow of Persephone weeds
that linger and ropes that ask which tree to
climb which branch to cling to for a summer
it's the eleventh hour when no candle burns
beyond the point of literature a maze of sounds
the lure of meaning and distress the end of all
that resembles whatever went before
leaves and shadows the length of porphyry
the fading dawn of erased fingers and cries
stifled by glyphs and unwoven shrouds
the first twelve minutes of eternity

11-08-20

THREE OF A KIND : THE DENSE PLURALITY OF MEMORY

i

MARY LOU IN A DREAM

"*Einmal
Lebt ich, wie Götter, und mehr bedarfs nicht*"
Hölderlin, An die Parzen

somewhere in the world it's Monday
fixed madrigals of ink and broken lyres
last night I dreamed my first love came to me
her sad countenance bereft of light
at least three moons were fading in the sky
and corn-fields frozen in their antiquity
stretched paling out beyond the highway
that goes to cities blazing at the fingertips
Eurydice I addressed her what unspoken word
has brought you here what accent what
rough aspiration unfulfilled what fuse
and seed that never bloomed what distance
a leaf a crown of withered ivy and echoes
the second or third syllables of a forgotten song
what discolors this unfound day no dawn hails
and hills replete with dun and ocher grief
we walked there once beads of pearly sweat
and fell deep into mythic earth embraced
no sound but breath that embroiders light
and now as the dead re-awaken in their thoughts
sent circling fluttering and yellowed rags
into the cosmos never to return you arrive
unsummoned a sequence of black suns your eyes

no glitter sparkling in your gaze just a lamp
gone out smoldering and a list of repercussions
mutations of memory at three in the afternoon
clocks suspended at the crossroads a voice
like rumors in a fading Spanish dialect
called out names we could not understand
adherence to a promise in unmown grasses
to the disjointed fingers of the planet Mars
sudden winters that disrobe the adolescent mind
dissolving what small divinity was being born
a chance to gain on the speed of metal
bright archaic of stolen and fermented kisses
you took my dreaming hands and weary
as dew departing from its marriage to the sun
you spoke to me of things I could not hear and
together we leaned looking out a window
to a future of curtained margins to woods
where lost souls wander in a labyrinth of poetry
leaves and letters none will ever read
inscriptions burning in the constancy of desire

11-09-20

ii
A MEMORY OF CLAIRE BIRNBAUM SUMMER 1958

how can decades of years be reduced to sand
directionless and volatile the passions of a single minute
a priceless brazier in the eye of sand distinct
from the seas and the oars and crowns of algae
the night orientations of shipwrecks of ghosts
lovers who spilled the wrong perfume in the wrong motel
a mirror of yellowing futures cracked because the comb
and the essence of hair and ink and the indissoluble
weeping of distant hills the very zones of loss
and longing that occur at the moment of death
neither before or after but precisely when the soul
knows that breath is an unpronounceable syllable
crystallized dew rock formations in the shape of poetry
the immense and illegible screen of fireflies and stars
radiating suspense and aphasia in the dormer
where doctor and munitions expert trade secrets
the entire cosmos pivoting on this exhilaration of physics
the island of Sicily tripartite and violent with lavas
and excoriations of ideals fumigation and lunacy
the very instant the soul sets forth into the vagaries
of a stairway of smoke to climb and ignore the shoulder
of rivers the massive undertow of memory the pearl
and jasmine painted on the eyelid's enormous interior
Israel of dreams assemblage of vowels uttered in
the manic absence of ritual the famous echo
redundant as stone in the middle of a bottomless pool
dialects of unreason stuttering amber of a rabbi

whose tongue bifurcates into hemispheres of oblivion
and then the names come rushing from the mind
the afternoons of consonants devoured by the insane
mouth the fix and the needle and the voyage to Inferno
on a single paddle boat to look for the Bride whose
very being is the isolation of all context and metaphor
beauty in the shimmering mirage of Eternal Return
hands in the shadow of time blessed for their inherent
loss and brooding and the Bride in circles of escape
and rumor assuming a nomenclature of philology
brilliant and evanescent the very nano-second when
life surrenders its grottos and shadows to the window
and the repercussions of glass and the lengthy noon
that extends its brief infinity into the veranda
of the black sun of the Aztecs and what's more
sand the dialectics of the wedding that took place
in the Far South of the citadel of intoxication and
inspiration the Nine Sisters colliding in cellophane skirts
and trumpets blessing the Bride wherever she may be !

11-10-20

iii
TRANSFORMATIVE VISION
the errors I have made recording the dates
of my so-called life the magenta and plasma
the inks in the margins destroyed by old typewriters
spoiled airs in the chamois and parchment of dialects
ruins of mountain crests and illusory hagiographies
the heights abandoned by Hesiod in the first instance
and to return to this remarkable day of reckoning
when brother and shadow parallel the tow-path
following the knees and shoulders of a stream
relegated to an oblivion of parsimonious willows
what's to recount of that moment when the sun
already ancient a hoary brain turning black
perched on the topmost step crowing raven-like
and brother and soul of shadow of brother
petrified in the calendar of non-existent days simply
transformed into instantaneous shimmering a shiver
on the hairline of light when it borders on darkness
the extinction of language and the absorption
of all thoughts into the diminutive medium of air
how many the quanta of memory around that dizzying
spell and brother and the highway as One fusing
tarantula and hyacinth and Toltec stone into
a colossal myth of cities that cannot ever Be
shedding hours shaking off the weeks of the Infinite
behold the noon the irreversible top spinning
the floor-boards shaking with primordial fear
each of the days marked for ascension and flame
divisible by three and the jazz of interruption

hundreds the folios of polyandry and pre-history
fuels and grammar of rooftop madness high forever
listening with the keen ear of isolated memories
bridge and topography of autumns rushing to take
the lawn by surprise and brother and soul of shadow
of brother rolling over and over down-slope
catch me by the hair ! Toynbee and Spengler
in pocket editions four pages long and theories
and mantras of the Invisible Pyramid the jungle
warp the titanic alluvial that buries all essence
what is greater than the Erased moment of time ?
by wending riverside and music of Dvorak and hoots
and hollers of phantom Lakota and buffalo spurred
by the steam engine of progress to desert the prairie
there we were on the flat-ledger of land plats and
counties colored all hues of the map on the very
margin of alternate realities feuding for possession
of the Mississippi valley and smoke architectures
the mind the multiplication of sleep the finale
of Neolithic symphony and vowels and hendecasyllable
school work tiny sums algebraic and Moorish puzzles
take it all away, Joe ! hedonism of the candy bar
and mid-afternoon soporific drug and languid
mournful Lady Day singing into a rhinoceros horn
it all goes away that instantaneous infinite shimmering
this strange day of reckoning this Joe and that Joe
suburban and gliding between Byzantine walls
porphyry and eglantine the prize brass music
floating waning disappearing in unconstructed clouds
the two of us soul and shadow on our backs
flim flam consonants star-stuff evanescent leaves
gathering with our eyes the remains of light
that day unregistered forgotten by everyone
when Joe had his *Transformative Vision*

11-10-20

THE PENUMBRA THAT SEPARATES TIME
FROM THE BREATH IT TAKES TO LIVE

the distances that separate sky from concrete
and man's wrath from his own longing
poetry of the immense spaces above and below
eye that only sees shadows and depth of clouds
the transitory nature of birth and eventuality
contained in a summation of glass and silence
repercussions of a single hand of a wave out of context
worlds speared by the hummingbird's iridescent beak
flight and death ! how inseparable they are
and you ask about the repetitions of a vowel
of a sound which escapes its own ladder of possibilities
language as an astronomical conjecture
phonetic laws extrapolated from asterisks and meteors
radiation of energy and thousands of green blades
attributed to a solitary finger lost in a maze and beside
the self the *other* self the poignant umbrella of thought
shedding a small darkness over the preliminary day
how can three possibly be a number ?
going over and over the same brief inch of breath
the distances become more remote the experience
of travel across a corridor of water and grief
direction itself pointed north rather than south realm of
those dead from the start who trace redundancies of name
with a pared thumb-nail and when will you ever
get it mythology of the coffin and its painted consonants
harmony married to the cosmic question displayed
in inks of reversal and quintessence of starry
houses that darken all too soon rooms and stairs
where the petty deities of the cigarette huddle
what is it that eludes you sleeping and in love ?
the anvil left to rust in yesterday's wheat field
where metaphors of wind and lightning abound
Romans and Trojans and Lazarus on the perimeter
where the poem leaves off and the mountain
square root of azure and indigo multiplied by zeta
enormous absences the *children !* penumbra
and lunation the voluble third heaven where
deceased leaves migrate and smaller yet echoes
that once widened the eyes of horses at dawn
come to rest in yearning distances of memory

I am too old to recall the rest and still you keep returning
in the unknown shape of an oracle buried in stone
help ! what ear is plausible enough to listen ?
and the remoteness between *ego* and *thou* ?
sleep of winged insects the inevitable quanta that
separate whatever cannot be from what never was
smoldering airs the vast and inflnite beyond

11-12-20

THE DAY MAX WENT TO THE HOSPITAL

ignorant of voice the heavens of number and sound
redound in the finite zero of memory echoes of shoulder
burdened with death and shape and tone of thumb
the resistant valley of yesterday's umbrage toiling
with woods come rushing to water's edge
surface where Narcissus and Lazarus return their
infinitesimal cries for salvation and do leaves changing hue
and stemming from a violent origin ever reside ?
autumnal resin and puerperal fever of metal
reflecting the absences of children the dread lock
of hair shorn at the wrong time the razor blade
in its plastic oblivion and the photo machine
gyrating in the dark sheaths of pre-dawn New York
how many cities encapsulated in the trembling azure inch
just above the aching formation of an unbuilt bridge
consonants heavy with old world haggling and fish
suddenly writhing in the nacre backdrop of an eye
just being born and distances ruddy with cupolas of love
the drained fuels of the addict on his concrete pallet
frozen to the double lake of transience and mercury
streets ! numbered and alphabetized and left to smolder
ruins of man's effort to overcome man and colors
of skyscrapers trembling in the avid rapacity
of the first sun to ever make it past the clock-tower
now only a blackening cinder a ray of uranium
pushed to the limit in the intensive care unit
where doctors learned in Turkish medicine perform
rituals that evoke secrets of the pyramid and gesso puppets
talking in the Indonesian dialect of the Ramayana
I had a son I had a son I had a son named Max I had a
repetitions and mourning and dove-cotes assassinated
by a heroin needle and purges of cooing and devotion
the stairs that never travel and the underground
with its speed of sound lurching through abyss of waters
refuse fruit without ardor junctions of sublime noise
features that never end in a quality of cloud and scum
threats that a new system will take cover and illustrate
painfully the loss of all credibility in the body politic
swarms of blind bees evicted from their frozen hives
a minotaur will appear on fifth avenue roaring
over the profound losses on the stock market
what is to survive ?

11-12-20

ARIADNE AUF NAXOS

the brain is a wasteland
the brain is a cemetery populated by those forgotten
by everyone else the dangerous left cheek
the foot that cannot be manipulated
the resident anger in hair
the illustrated weeklies tossed out the window
glass and forceps and words that linger
in syllables of smoke the genius
of retardation and disused coinage
on and on the perimeters and parameters
a junkyard of heaped atrocities in paper and crayon
ching ching ching of dead cash registers
me for you and the bad opium deal
perfume that destroys the girlfriend's skin
how archaic is the face found upside down
in a pool of asbestos and quicklime
there are reasons the moon has turned to ruddy dust
pale a wasting fiction of fragrances and detritus
it is insects especially that are heroic
cicadas who multiply July going blind
fireflies who mistakenly forge skies of glowing litmus
a wonder that bees and dragon-flies perpetuate the sun
containing in its vast arc the music of distance
the brain is a wasteland a virtual copy of water
of remote control units opposed to thumbs
is there a cause for love in insectaries and hives ?
marshlands of sleep where *Ariadne* wanders
trussed between gramophone horn and clepsydra
how sound is the orient of her only note !
maddened by penitents staggering on a single shoe
Song of Destiny ! children are but homophones
of silence the mutual distinctions of flight and loss
the brain is a cemetery where woebegone
the Trojans inter the best of their insect hordes
then what am I ? the book-of-the-dead walking
all the way from Philadelphia to Potsdam
a cemetery for unknown languages and oracles
rock formations that spell the end of time
seas of hollow bottoms and yearning
how deep the sky is tonight duplicated
at all right angles and a flaring cusp
I have been to indigo and sought the Nymph
whose hair is awash in a metaphysics of leaf and noise
winds that scour acres in a pantomime of grief
corn shocks tied to the rudder of a ghost ship
the brain is a wasteland of things that cannot be dreamed
whose eye-socket is repercussion of clouds
an afternoon theater whose actors are locusts
the trident of salvation spears their diminutive sight
I am the lack in the hollow of the hour
an organ-grinder is weeping his street

the very outside of the mind is a futility of vowels
when monkey comes home the god Bacchus is to blame
Ariadne ! islands come and go and enormous heat
and the circles envisioned by the Ionians yesterday
courtroom evidence the universe is fake
when did two sisters ever equal ?
a wasteland a cemetery a brain a destitution
of reason and history a shifting paralysis of light
two lamp fixtures revolving like deaf planets
how is anything ever to be remembered ?
is this the voice
       that broke the arrow
              that flew from the shaft
                     that promised a memory of stone ?

11-13-20

BODAS DE SANGRE : MEMORY OF NIKKI ARAI

around the corner from the bookstore where we worked
was a bar open all afternoon where we mixed
and drank whiskey sours or gin and tonics until
the day had lost all its repercussions and the cigarettes
distributed by the gods and the smoke of love and fasting
and virtually the excitement of alcohol at 3 PM
exchanged identities the Armenian became the Far East
and shoes and elbows clinked and clanged a soldered
air attached to metal exhausted from its retail price
difficult to shine and yet her face your face the moon
that only appears in bars in the afternoon a bonsai
that drifts through the eyes your eyes drifted and
forsaken your child somewhere in the keep of frost
and the spirit-nurses of Fujiyama how could we
have known holding the bone relics of the Buddha
while we lost all attention to detail letting blurred
contours of cloud and eclipse fog our nascent religion
bookkeeping of deities the silken essence of thought
your skin with its utter aphasia and blinking behind
a mirror the force of your identity about to shatter
form and reason in the lap of Mercy the blood-letting
of the future in numerous hotels and photography
workshops the whole mess that was to become no sooner
had we left the city of Chicago to sink into its Lake
double the hemisphere that throbbed in your left temple
the train ride to the Southside on straw mats and
a reading of the Lotus Sutra for example looking
out windows that somehow contained the shore of Time
as short as the skewered glance of the physicist who
might assure us space had little chance in the debacle
of birth and death the tiny digits spinning I was in love
totally with my veins heated by 80 degree alcohol

promises made to meet clandestine suitcases and
still the astrology of the hive of cramped darkness
where on a mattress on the bare floor you exposed
not only the massive skeins of your ink-length hair
but your wounds and departure of the senses naked
and raw as my backside after you had whittled it
with signatures stolen from red Chinese ink-blocks
how did it all occur on such an obscure calendar date ?
soon it was a different decade and the sun defeated
by its own retrograde homophone and night especially
we called it *Bodas de Sangre* in the Durant Hotel
the library was capsized into its own decimal system
and a water was out there incorporating reflections
of all the possible moons captured in your camera lens
we copied each other we invented Lazarus and his
telephone we dialed and spun and crashed in intimacy
of careers and kaleidoscopes and *you* finally not
in the anonymous bar but in a square unit of General
Hospital an entire afternoon away and no way to
fix it the passion the gods dealt out that faulty hour of
smoke and raw gin and knee rubbing knee hands
like braids of hair reaching under the table *Love*

I confess this was the experience as I recall it
glyphs and stitches and perfumes *the* Opium

11-13-20

BALLAD OF THE ALL BUT FORGOTTEN
"la eternidad vulnerable de las fotografías"
                              Lorca

as for life it's what is already gone
enough of the lascivious mansions of vanity
the plus signs before the hue and print
the eye throbbing to the left of the wall
whole margins of the sun blown away by
a single vowel attitudes of a river run
dry in the smoke of the hour a life what
is it but collapsed huts & rattling sistra
a broken wheel found in a rain-ditch
masks discarded paper-weights and mirrors
trapped reflections in tarnished glass
one more breath the constellations in
their eyes exploding silently drained of
flame as for life it's a white burnout a
thought without repercussions a drone
in the left ear a buzz and a chisel and
a hammer taken to the knee a hive
of frozen wax full of fossil bees exo-
skeletons cigarettes and distances ruddy
and fading fused to dun the hills like
mind-dust driven drift drizzle opaque
But just for a minute stop and listen
to the child inert beneath the thumb-nail
turning brown as insects immured in
a parenthesis of water and metaphor
cries in ultra-violet and clouds woven
into the hyacinth of his eyes and
an urgent Apollo god of Mice who rails
daily against man's repetitions to man
sending shafts and burial notices and
why is this important this outline in *amarillo*
of an unrecorded biography and Listen
again to the tone of the ear the marooned
philosophy redundant in abandoned shoes
what is the blank and stop and the market
where lice and onions and the insanity
of consonants vying for speed and air
what is reversed in the album of light
almost nothing when towers of noise
and sepulchers of red ants and the terrific
gust of a wind that passes through stone
the child ! nameless ephebe in azure
ragged sleeves and lawns and threes
what letter is sewn inside his *right* eyelid ?
ten is never fifty ! what surpasses an inch
in death ?

11-14-20

HUNAHPÚ and XBALANQUÉ

remains nameless the thing before birth
iridescence of unseen stars and asterisks
texts of space in all its pristine nudity
fire devouring fire in the effort to overcome
the fixity of time as it surges in all directions
polar attitudes to destroy and create north
and south the winds that bear away seeds
emerges from stone thought primordial
music in the hollows of rock below the sea
skies redundant in their echoing sublimity
shaking furiously empires of shapeless cloud
do rains then commence and lightning bolts
and summers that last four thousand months
how does passion evolve from the blind worm's
distant shadow the sudden dawn of birds
circling in the pack-animal's enormous eye
mountain computes mountain in ghazals
of unlettered longing the origins of vowels
and voices of entropy and cosmic metaphor
round and round the unheard note strikes
its camphor and brassy isotopes and moons
the size of ink the length of sand scatter
through the eastern smokes of age and death
scorpions magenta and violet carry the sun
blackened by its youthful fever into pools
of marginless hematite where enormous statues
drink with their weapons and newly minted wheels
burning with eternal ardor to move and resound
clash in the vibrating instant of consciousness
continents the perimeter of aleph zones of mind
apprehending but not understanding the why
of creation's glottal stop and unfurled banners
of ether and radial symmetries red dusts fists
fierce allusions to an alternate system of thinking
jargons of grass and leaf innocence of ears
laid to the ground listening to water rush
through the apex and nadir of infinity
how often will this start without ending ?
punctuations that dazzle the firmament even
as it slides off the spatial skin into a loss
of memory and a calibration of countless eons
you and I somewhere in the middle of oblivion
hemispheres of colloidal recall and depths
to live ! the divine *once* determined to *be*
similitude to the *other* an evaporating reflection
in the amazing reticulation of gravity
shifts of accent and tone in afternoon's fading
the two of us dots squiggles hues of remote
the colloquy of sperm and entelechy heights
the hand obtains searching for shape and meaning
the end zone the zodiac of illustrated matter

issuing from the brain at the moment of recovery
the instant that is both before and after
neither three nor its lack dissolved forever
what we always were walking home backwards

11-15-20

THE BOOK I NEVER WROTE

what is the real title of this book ?
who are the authors of each of the titles
of this book ? what cannot be contained
in this book will not be read and lest
germinations of extra vowels occur or letters
other than those consigned to potters' field
what is the subject of this tome this text
this codex this sky-image this pool of lost
thoughts was it ever intended or can it
be cataloged or assigned a unit number
a cipher a hue a disposition toward the divine
or merely a list of words designating bird-
flight pinnacle mountain heap or dust bin
cannot question its why or wherefore like
an atlas or almanac the version of each
season changed with new days divided
by the number of subtracted hours or are we
confused by the proportion of heaven to
the direction of gravity and decorated with
mercury and metaphor semantics relegated
to an index with series of deities long on
consonants to pronounce as the afterthought
dictates italics and Romanization to the
contrary as are opposable thumbs and grief
the admixture of potting soil omissions
of dream-spell interpretations as footnotes
and shadows of tears mourning the greater
loss the vanishing horizons and verbiage
at sunset hills disappear and voices eerie
ululations lunar signals in the branches
held above dew-fall hardening of myth
in stone rock under water resonance inky
shale and gravel each a foot away from time
until inches from the thumb a lever shifts
all red explodes the retina talking silence
wandering syllables missing pagination
the library in a match-box from beta to
gamma illegible sections in glyphic contact
going up and down the cigarette stepping
gingerly aside or at the top where only
half visible or legible alphanumeric plates
holding close to the glass the glosses few

as they are and finally if a conclusion can
be and diverse sources indicate future
markets jettisoned noises from the bark
chiseled liquids oars rampant assonance
and does *he* matter the suspected author
the candid silhouette locked to his wall
of darkness the subject and object of ego
the longing in the loam the worm increased
by its own diminution *him* matter ? style
and fusion the terrific silence of drums
rolling through memory's ethereal house
harbors of illusion Homer and pre-Socratics
doing song with the Phrygian cap worn
on the nameless body tossed into dogs' ditch
him too handless at the ruptured helm a
diphthong of distance from what the ear
entails falling asleep in the midst of the text
syllables of oneiric volume the weights and
measures of sound dropping from syntax
in the end just the leaf burdened by recall
of its voice murmuring in the stars

11-16-20

QASIDA

I wake up on the moon
what hour is it ? cuckoos rouse
and sun reaps early harvest
my love is a loss in dust and wheat
a summer curtailed by locust hordes
memory no more than tinfoil wrapped
around something long discarded
my love is an hour on the moon
what month is it what verse
soundless rhymes edges of vowels
lingering assonance of silver
and mercury and all the while earth
that deformed little digit going around
the sun now big and ripe and dark
in the eternal air of poetry
and my love on the other end
of the telephone and Lazarus doing
his walk-about in the down under
and the streets of dew and silence
waking now to aromas of freshly
baked breads and a patina of humus
could my love be the sound
of grieving at curb's edge ?
whispers that bring down gravity
and houses marooned by their hair
did a single drop of water
destroy the ear in its echo ?
how much the shoulder hurts
this moment between lives
I have a face that's lived too long
and hands that anchor themselves
to grasses mown in haste
yet my love is the invisibility
that marks an end to arrow's flight
the slightest inch beside the light
that ekes its existence out
in the moon's final fading phase

11-16-20

THE ORIGINS OF POETRY

the exactly what was it about the first verse
the time between stone and the unknown grass
walked in meters sidestepping into a mansion
the dwelling of emptiness and lyre and resound
the fictitious goddess pale in her moon of transience
hotels then and approach the way snaking through
ivy and gravel night in garages reeking of alcohol
and stale gasoline did the lamp waver as new planets
unnamed sources of thought edges of the spatial
discourse shattered and brilliant talking over
cigarettes and bottles half full and lacquered
chandeliers above the head to make divine the small
moment of discovery followed by an oblivion
of centuries lay down the head on its rock and myth
longing for the absence of *one* shimmering at
the bed-head sections of purity carved from air and
celestial repercussions in the ear somnolence
of the library unopened indexes and a pyramid
darkening with the age of green and did shine ! once
gods fulminant with adolescent rage come to see
peering over the canyon's rim into a polyglot
acre of clover the love of first dialects and a body
imagined to be *her* as ancient and modern as
words that have lost meaning but sounds the sublime
an instantaneous glyph photo-montage going
through the stages all of life from birth the inter-uterine
memory when seas had legs and raced the chasuble
of time to a smoking end echoes and drizzle of fire
earths in collision if opium and its suburbs and
one morning of a summer in the Park waking
you assemble the shrapnel of a dream and call
names out you never knew and hence the poem
with its phantom legends spills forth a beam
a ray a shining before the opaque leaf that
shapes itself against the dormant glass
yearning for a vowel to define it
a breath a voice

11-17-20

I ESPY DIANA *ON THE CHASE IN THE DUSKY HILLS OF ETRURIA*

negligent of garb her shoulders bare
a dross of mercury in her eye
a battered clip a-dazzle in the broken sun
holds together the flimsy deep-dyed cloth
once forest green now a faded lunar stale
incoherent of speech her mumbling tongue
some prayer advances toward the skies
redundant in their opalescence and rumble
of clouds deters nothing of her fleet-of-foot
wayward through vale and chasm and painting
she is the subject half-tones and twilight hues
against the opaque luster of her skin
itself the tempt and frailty of her being
a slight perspiration pearls paths
over the dimensions of her divine shining
a brightness once her presence and hair unkempt
its ribbons tattered or tossed to zephyrs
of a lost summer and if words resemble
something of speech on her breath of last
night's many cigarettes does she at all waver
does the quiver sliding off her back does
anything about her in torn denim
an indecency clings to her loping gait
over submissive lawns of dead Tuscan senators
and heads straight to the hummock
to take aim did not some darting hummingbird
break the rectilinear force the fierce
recall suddenly of a paramour she disdains
or to a stag changed whom she will kill
and more beautiful than transformations
of a water more echo than light
she trembles a shiver of immortality
as she balances the rock on which she stands
and Lo the ancient source of darkness
her envelopes and hides from mortal sight
her absolute and instantaneous Being
a painting a shimmer an elocution of air
powders of infinity a shower of cold flame
erased forever from the poet's mind
Diana who comes and goes in verses
of unheard sound a trill of dawning thought
a vowel of plangent leaves

11-17-20

INFATUATION

> "Aconteceu-me do alto do infinito
> Esta vida …"
> Fernando Pessoa

i

I introduce the door to its shadow
and in comes the bride-to-be
from some foreign land beyond
this peppered and fevered clime

offers me the rose of her smile
shakes hair blessed by distant dews
says something in a tongue I cannot
comprehend and goes back out the door

rains it does in this and other cities too
sidewalks flood with desiccated petals
my heart is the drum on which pound
the rain's million tiny fists

ii

comes a time we all must leave here
numbed by the passage and metaphors of time
I have wandered and lost and wandered and lost
I have been to Havana and Barcelona
and traveled as far as Ladakh where
        the mountains kiss the sky
I have affixed pronouns to the leaves
and listened to the doormen and twice-born
discourse on grief from the loss of a son
I have listened to the Hindustani song
        about the Wheel of rebirth
yet found silence of salvation only in the stone
and written poems from lessons of the trees
        that do not grow from pride and envy
and loved I have and twice as many times
and heard the accounts of seers multiply
the numbers which death contains
and stopped by the steward's chambers
where rock-hewn lions await their coronation
and journeyed to the south of heaven
where inverted pyramids promised to return
        my brother's stolen shadow
from on high where the infinite battles
with its unborn inch I have peered
asleep with the mastodons of thought
giving little credence to the spinning worlds
and myths of organization and triumph
a smaller day an hour less than half its size
night-times in the revel of forbidden kisses
the sensation that tomorrow is the last of all

that fretting over index and thumb-nail
or the shallow pool where immersed my face
     forges its own oblivion
Infatuation ! the bonds that chain us to breath
the living cipher that empties great hotels
scars and lesions and the panoply of skin
the shining adjectives that decorate a poem
or the derivative vowels of the secret consequence
repercussions of water and memory !
and yes I have been to the undertaker
surveyed the cemeteries on the hill
and pressed the green cremation button
yet learned nothing of the score

iii

how is it the divine has no shape
and knee and shoulder burdened
by the press of imperious gravity
have no solution but to mourn ?

torn between two languages and
misunderstood in the dialect of time
aphasia and monumental statuary
blindness of marble in the noonday sun

who was the girl who came and went
a sheaf of corn a sprig of lilac in the wind
hands that flowered in the dark
smile that dissolved in the endless rain

infatuation all that the eye beholds a leaf
shaking off its noun in soundless eternity

11-18-20

THE INTERRUPTED CONSCIOUSNESS

light cut short before day's end
stalemate of the hours in a microscope
looking out from the vestiges of time
behold the lens held backwards and flight
of migratory beings souls and birds alike
reversed in a collapsed sky of cellophane
ridges dominated by paper flowers
etched in an x-ray of a questionable deity
echoes fractured by ammonium and ether
as the body goes under a sea of weights
nocturnal animals on the prowl at noon
scavenging in the pronominal abyss
something lost a hand a finger a blade
the reunion of minds scheduled for three
postponed to an oblivion of grass growing
in the brief inch still possible of thought
on a throne of burning nouns memory
struggles to free itself from rock fragments
statues clepsydras shifting walls minor
abscesses hiatus of Greek letters swarms
of bees hovering on the edge of language
punctuation of sound without meaning
the ear jams with a repercussion of air
water becomes a mere rumor behind
the hairline a conjecture without origins
landfall gravel underfoot rubber tires
skidding by cliff's edge if only if only
reaching up from a miasma of bed-clothes
sheets wrapped around the tiny vowels
of error and the grand and futile yawn
of clouds anchoring in the window
such a distance to the feet !
slowly the fogs of interruption rise
taking the knees by surprise then
capsizing hips and the solemn rites
of the heart puzzled by oracular noises
a stethoscope listening for winter
though outside the circular heats of summer
and a traffic of metal and shining horns
tubular destinies vagaries of a mountain
that has lost touch with the heavens
ever more remote the lawns shifting
from view with their scattered toys
a kite drifting into the ozone
darkening leaves of voice
gone silent

for Max

11-19-20

ORPHEUS WITHOUT SONG

"E eu sonho sem ver
os sonhos que tenho"
Fernando Pessoa

was seen wandering dazed in the wood
a young man unknown and apparently
someone escaped from an unfinished epic
if questioned only looked askance and
pulled at the cords around his waist
and asked again who just defiantly
stared at the new rising sky and with
alarm shaking hands a finger indexed
to trembling in the grass pointed dark
the thing none could see a dream perhaps
the vision of an errant soul exiting by
accident from one of three possible heavens
or hell the worst conjecture could hear
if listened well the syllables whispered
from lips cracked the hemispheres of
reason discounted or approached with
caution his peering eyes what color of
distant hills they were a solemnity and
sorrow fitting the nature of his malady
a deformation of consonants like the rumor
of water the ascension suddenly of the
lunar orb shed little light on his body
was eerie the spectacle him gazing into
the leafage the borrowed splendor of
an unexpected day a noon or some shift
of hue in the spectrum of sleep his voice
a clamor of silence in the rustling maze
and then as onlookers watched he
took his shadow and vanished

11-20-20

MORTON ARBORETUM
for clyde flowers

more to be said cannot and as the sheep
fell into the eyes and drowsy splendors washed
from the terse final sky an autumn wind a
vagary and longing in the upraised branches
yearning for an even deeper red a more profound
ocher we went driving through the park unable
to count our years though young we must have
been memory bifurcating without a trace a
left wing in the heavens the right wing a vessel
of drained air the hypothesis of a former life
we stopped to stain the wind with our fingers
wet with wine or a verse from the *Rubaiyat*
which we really didn't understand the lace
fringes of an enormous cloud formation shaking
in our ears a vowel incandescent vibrated long
until darkness the evidence of what cannot be
named took us by our knees and then tumbling
we heard without wanting the voices proclaiming
the separate quarters of hell the vagabond soul
the demon who would a deity be and other choruses
a jazz of disparate hemispheres bright and remote
even as the night of leaves descended covering
this patch of earth the forest preserve on the
outskirts of town as they say the motor stalled
we awaited the signal from planet Mercury and
silence the dishevelment of space and breath

11-20-20

AN AFTERNOON WITH MIRCEA ELIADE
UNIVERSITY OF CHICAGO 1958

the daily intransigence what's an apparatus
a code to defy the past its merits a fissure
in the outer ramparts of space where light
collides with light being reborn and dying
in reverse and did I tell you about the trans-
formation of desires the annulled passions
the grasses that lay down mourning and dew
in all its splendid architecture a maze of unseen
and spectacular repercussions the ear cannot
nor the eye transcend their properties a fuel
and a patronymic at the verge of phonetic
corruption the deal is this to whittle away
at the life-source reciting the ineffable sounds
of archaic mantras the Vedas a procurement in
the courts and yet it's all noise a radio that won't
turn off microchips the brain itself rattling on in
a cuneiform dialect thoughts about star-stuff lunar
derangements summer showers cloud-bursts all in
the mind going on and on trying to decipher exactly
what is meant by the oracular syllables emanating
from planet Jupiter no less and furthermore the thing
hidden in the lawn the lack of shining when Dawn
tears apart the fabric and talking as if the hydrants
and fountains and other origins of water the great
molecules of hydrogen and you know whatever science
has to teach us and afterwards in small groups
holding hands walking and ambling and heading
straight to the drugstore and the sun a slanting
toward the west where hills now occupy the horizon
can remembrance of these afternoons like pages
of a chemistry textbook be so easily forgotten ?
being is not to grasp the *other* is still inexplicable
mooning over lost loves sliding briefly but forever
into insanity pounding the walls for a clue what's
the story ? splitting the atom under the bleachers
while some bonze goes on about Aristotle and
the middle ages upon us and flight into the ozone
hummingbird and pyramid childhood in a single
instant past the road that leads to the lake whose
surface rippled by a small maelstrom of ideas and
so forth you get the point
quietly slowly without acrimony the *leaf* darkens
without seeing without recording simply night
as it descends in endless waves of oblivion
a dream of seas unfolding bottomless
or of stone in eternal silence

11-21-20

OF POETRY...

being and time thought and disorder
for every cubic inch of gravity the ear
must endure a word loses meaning and
only sounds revolve pointlessly going
into the ether that alternate sphere where
oracular disorganization and stone dominate
a lyricism of death and silence the rent
fabric of last summer's cloud and rain
that lasts longer than memory the very
and even and air and light and breath
summoned by the dark finger of some deity
vowels placed in no special order nightmare
and fugue of consonants and lips cracked
and brawls of a nocturnal world the real
and only when lovers separate in agonies
best measured in hexameter and longing
the oblivion of rebirth and the brief
instant of water in all its repercussions
from which arise the Muses or the goddess who
Haunts and pastels and months of bright
and yet the sun with its black homophone
reverses the direction of mind and night
brings on with a stellar malignancy and
the only true subject is *loss* irrecuperable
laid out in hieroglyphs that tattoo coffins
and the Father of the underworld lifts his
hoary head into the sparkle demanding
his bride the flower-footed Nymph sheathed
in emblem and meter the leaves that *talk*
and the furrows where spears are born
and warriors in a language more ancient
than the sea itself storms of emotion ire and
jeopardy and rushing blindly a repetition
of marble until noon the profligate hour
when heat and statues suffer migraines
and hands foremost shapeless seeking
the outline of a prosody of fingers and rumor
so much ! so very much to deny ! loud !
it is only antiquity with its cut veins and
pottery of red geometries *Islands* hush
terrible and irreversible inch of recognition
Sanskrit parrot deleting all sense with its
famous and beautiful parti-colored beak
dialect of burning shafts and footfalls
that none but the *poet* can apprehend
a nuisance of adultery noise and beauty
chiaroscuro of the soul *darkest* thing
in the body
is night the same as sky ?

11-22-20

KINDERTOTENLIEDER
  "paśya, Mādhava, me sutam"*
            Mahabharata

not *the* sea but fragments of *a* sea
as dead of year approaches the approximate
stillness of all time pivoting on a single dot
evanescent immemorial when hour plunges
hour in a surf of gloom and skies become nil
the abscess of oblivion cloud-tossed red-rimmed
horizon vanishes from the astral map
chill of human endeavor mothers and lapwing
kestrel and osprey shrill ululations wings
dappled with sea-spray mind going over
itself in a music of silent repercussions
how is it ? will it ever ? and the unheard
drum-roll cold incandescence of the heart
the rest is too familiar streets notched by smoke
hazard of sleep tensions between the chariot
and the horse hospitals repeated at dawn
windows which are the resting place of souls
the abracadabra of mourning not suitable
for language of any sort the books piled up
on each other willy-nilly dog-eared pages
scribbled notes jotted down in a fever
the release of the body from its shadow
or is it the other way around reversal
of all objects in the mirror taciturn matter
drawers half-opened where clothes remember
the limbs they once fit and skipping from ear
to ear the wayfaring song of children
who have been removed from the register of names
mere syllables now wafting in the darkened ether
night folded in on itself a starry waste of
notes plied by an invisible harp the legends
that encompass stone and the rumor of water
the stairway the memory of a stairway and
summer littered in tiny particles of heat
over a once splendid tapestry of colored pebbles
a rushing without feet a nuance of hands
dew transient in the absence of light
what was ! what *ever* was ! leaves torn from
the shapes of words sounds without meaning
ever fast in the dead of time the brief cries
a noise of eaves dripping dark echoes
silence
            "look at my boy now, Madhava"

11-23-20

APPENDIX VERGILIANA

soft the ever falling in the ear sleeping
final distance the echo of an unexamined vowel
was the time you wanted to but couldn't
pronounce and stuttering to no avail
the music discordant and sibylline dance
between perspectives of past and present
the erogenous hemisphere of space looming
over the unfinished half a puzzle with so much
depending on the parapet where the shadow
wavers in its paroxysm of being the *other*
and from afar the rumor of mountains collapsing
water shallow and infinite rippling echoes
a drift of light a splinter the moon excavated
from its shell of dreams a fraction of infinity
the size of a thumbprint the toga and brim
learning to walk again despite the aphasia
and drugged consonants each on the side
of the oracle as if clouds remnants of thought
wandering mind oasis of memory nothing lasts
the technique of meaning and the visible
which you discount unless it is opium or a horizon
flooded with an alternative to light the grasp
of unseen deities thirsty for knowledge of mortality
undergone the knife the running rivers of
darkness the mutilated sky threatening
you in a theater of lost months a brother
to no one but the shadow in error at your side
did you remember to read your lesson ?
night the cascade of ancient stars and a finger
to the left of time a situation of illegible
consequences you forge an idea which
lacks perimeters and saddened with grief
despond of the late afternoon's penumbra
going round to the back door to visit
the screen of fireflies consulting the display
as if it were an augur's promise the intent
to wake if possible the following day given
the discrepancy of hours and the recall of grass
sloping lawns mysterious houses clad in ivy
windows and dormers and gabled rooftops
the noise of the sibyl in her fly-green bottle
alert to the way the poem is supposed to begin
a start to arms and the man and the height
where a copy of Jupiter seems to hover
come noon and the equestrian marbles learning
to perspire and dread the eternity that
precedes the drone of bees wasted with desire
so you come to *this* the edge of reason
labyrinthine remembrance of cliff and sea
the vast below of the firmament the abysmal
chaos that separates leaf from leaf
husks of words and nothing more

11-24-20

DEAD OF NIGHT

"Ser poeta não é uma ambição minha
É a minha maneira de estar sozinho"
       Alberto Caeiro (Fernando Pessoa)

the frieze drilled into the sky a ruin of figurines
glyphs and punctuations passing so swiftly
from consciousness the losses and sorrows
light itself eclipsed from the least vowel and
the long echo of the last deity to *remember* anything
between heaven and earth wings of flight unseen
hasp and husk of noise injuries of thought
ascribed to the relics of statues surrounding
the lake of eternal obscurities murmurs of silence
hands erased from gravity sense and motion
all at a standstill in the intransigent traffic of stars
nocturnal clusters of myth burning inside a sleep
of rock and grass with indefinite articles
a stairway and cigarettes still lit and brass
announcing the ungodly Hour and the asbestos
of impermanence a rush to get home a longing
to get past the moment of one's life just to
enter the next one as if to avoid grief and larger
moments beside a huge water where pronouns
details in worn fabric plunge into the unfathomable
& grain gathered at month's end by the park
where by dawn bloom roses and dahlias zinnias
and begonias the faint line that divides this death
from the last in an obscure procession of lawns
and to espy the boat distantly one sail at a time
what ! the immemorial sea divides into fractions
inches from the source of consciousness and to
toss a pebble following its ripple across to
the other shore where trident in hand Neptune half-
adrift threatens to end the cinema darkening
remains of the arena where back and forth persons
assigned to names the *you* and the *me* enact
famous but forgotten scripts of archaic youth
surging from the depths up to a primordial footfall
phases of the moon evenings descend like powders
parallel paths a whistle in the gloaming a tiny
whiteness the resemblance to a voice looking
for a body to bear us to the grave which is our
vocation the tilde placed above the consonant
that stands for the finality of sound
in the dead of night

11-25-20

HERCULES

what can be louder than the sun ?
black homophones of light ! death beyond death
the remains of the beginning of nothing
metaphysics of noise sensational thoughtless
who can sleep on the borders of the sun ?
does Hercules advance clad in raw hides
only to lift the empty sky on his shoulders
and step with glee into the ruins of water ?
it is only in dying we surpass ourselves
infinite moment of regret a music that ascends
silently from the loss of breath the reckoning
of poetry and similes and metaphors
the hundred vowels and twice the number of consonants
employed to define that primordial and constant *Bang*
the boomerang of theory and astrophysics
how can consciousness suffer this delay of print ?
every star is the possibility of a hand a longing
for form and shape a yearning for stone
and grass a legendary moment of anticipation
backwards and front in the glass of perpetuity
the child within beholds the greater fragment of fire
and at once the dozens of copies of Hercules
manifest in all children roaming over a landscape
of interrupted sleep and warnings and
the long afternoon when eternity vanishes
by five o'clock and the scattered images of air
the fractions of cloud and intaglios of memory
shatter repeatedly and no one is immune
to this momentous oblivion the strength of the sun
in all its intensity of thumb and vertigo
where is the *Eye* that can see through and beyond
the anfractuous and aphasic solar syllables ?
Hercules burning in his own skin !

11-25-20

EL OLVIDADO

half way up the hill and down again
fourteen days and fourteen nights
asleep dense as stone in a deep well
dark the refulgent curve disappearing
behind a single dawning leaf green
and tender as dew about to evaporate
comes the hour to rise eyes wide open
to the scales where souls are balanced
does the pharaoh too rise shouting ?
sand returns to its origin and what
lies beneath the ancient soil a home
with rooms that go on forever and
the number three carved in thought
circling the various inch of sky high
in the festooned summer drone of bees
whose *brother* is on the keep waiting
for the inventions of Lazarus to work ?
whose *shadow* by the side of water
puzzled that it remains separated from
the promised body and yet exclamations
and foreclosures and bird-songs mantic
that shimmer like a noiseless sound
in the vestigial brain if only memory
could be so vivid and the great grass
that comes rushing down the slope
bearing with it the spit and ivory
of statues dominated by a shivered
chisel and the oracular vowel of ink
the deity lurking inside the spool
unwinding the profits of fate who
spends as much on sorrow as on
the small efforts of speech that go
into the Unseen cloud never to be
repeated but for the *brother* still
adrift a silhouette in glass darkening
and the shifts of wind the enigmatic
crevices where unused words go
syllables no ear retains nor recalls
in the labyrinthine foliage of night

11-26-20

THE RIDDLE OF BIRTH

on the other side of Never
where a shining Jesus strays
spoils are writ in molten gold
and waters run backwards
into the burning eye of grief
on the opposite shore of space
cuneiforms promise renewed light
and children shout manacled
by noises they cannot understand
and the useless vestige of echo
like the unmastered consonant
seems to linger buried in stone
an ear a fossil a tendril on the wall
the endless game of bright and cloud
the storm just beneath the bed
how many infancies in the shop
and window displays of death
that offer remote pasts to beings
without form or memory
on the unseen side of Never
where baby Krishna swallows time
a mountain of archaic blue
and a stillness like the end of grass
and rhymes that have no sound
a world that cannot come to pass
in the remains of a summer day
the shapes of unknown words
a poetry of speechless leaves
and hands that reach but do not
feel and the single finger lopped
off at the rim and the darkness
crying in the forbidden well
how far it is from *there* where
distance is consumed by longing
and *mother* is a hidden name
an hour in the labyrinth
a vision from before sky
was formed and sleep a glass
that lacks its other side

11-26-20

THREE SONNETS TO USHER IN THE DARK SEASON

i

for grief hit the insert tab and watch
the clouds scud away all yellow distant
sitting there on the nod a crescent filter
of remote flame the size of your brain
and print to excess the silences the vows
to never return to forget what once seemed
wild whose hair spurned the rules of concord
the gesso plated runway the shades of ink
and hit control release and words lose shape
sounds become alternatives of gravity until
a weightlessness sets in and the page transfers
its litany of untrammeled punctuations and
what is there to do but weep as the glass
assumes the trembling myth of unborn rock

ii

once is quite enough of breath the inanity
of trying to shape air with hands that belong
to someone else a brother whose seventy-second
autumn never came and there dwelling on songs
and inconstancy of echo the letters form and
fall apart spacing mountains on a molten page
what ! why you cannot comprehend the season's
over-valued tax-system the forlorn equations
that subject number to a water without reflections
light beams render nil the force of omega which
is just a vowel and not the end of all poems
you stammer with knees unlocked the cathedral
of your shoulders bent in a mute backspace
and it all comes apart light breath leaf and stone

iii

so remain the ruins of thought encumbrances
that issue from the abyss of words oracular dissension
of sound and stress that locks the winds in darkness
hold the shift key and see the skies re-form their
memory and hills where dialects learn to mourn
do such moments exist just to emphasis the print
demand of things destined to vanish forever
straddle the broken bridge the isthmus floats
into its own reverie of fallow land frozen fields
where corn-shocks dried rattle in oblivion
no recall of the summer spent in a single instant
crickets and hummingbirds and heat dyed red
like the lipstick of a goddess whose intent it was
to smoke one last cigarette and disappear

11-27-20

NOTE FOUND IN A BIBLE IN AN ABANDONED MOTEL ON THE OUTSKIRTS OF WHAT WAS ONCE REFERRED TO AS CITY-OF-ANGELS

tassels of light adorn the brow of time
think of it ! as a stone captures all sounds around it
so with eyes broken with grief the ancient soul within
clamors not for the body but for the body's shadow
the archaic dissemination of forms as ideas high
in the air circulating like planets and the immensity
of light as it emerges from the black vacuum of
eternity embraces us unimaginably unconscious
from the outset—do you remember ? hand to
mourn finger to sorrow grasses bend in a copy
of the rain that descends in sleep and for once and
only the pronominal moment of birth undertakes
a blind voyage through woods and plaintive groves
who will ever recall that passage through the labyrinth ?
and gods grown idiotic with pride and age set
traps and lure the dumb mortal to seizures of ecstasy
and death and ages roll by in an instant and Lazarus
ascends to invent the telephone and the corn-field
and listen to voices underneath the plight of Pluto's
Bride the white-clad spirit of six-month duration
and you too on the Library steps folding and unfolding
the Map of stars and cities that only exist in the mind
and such as it was the day fled taking with it a ravel
of skirts and cigarettes and some Latin quotations
exhausted at the top step you gave warning the lift
of a sigh the breath taken but never released
and skies opalescent and tiny racing like storms
summer in the second glance and a photograph
showing us both together and forever separated
how much greenery in the woven ear of memory !
puzzled with the hundred ambiguities of living
we took to poetry and astrology and the various
sciences of the vowel and consonant and lunar echoes
a scheme of meter and footfall the most ancient verse
blindly repeated into sleep's immemorial rock-den
could we but wake again together !
which of us would be the word and which the leaf !
tassels of light adorn the brow of time

11-28-20

THE SYRIAN GODDESS

afflicted already by the oncoming obscurity
in the broken marbles the principle a fragment
of cloud occluding with despair her eyesight
a day at a time drunken Roman legionnaires
sprawled out in the dust the variety of formations
arm and hip and bust erect and polished once
the prayers suffocating in a shattered Semitic dialect
up from old Babirush or farther east where eternal
fires fan the plateaus with brazen cuneiform figurines
watering spots camels dehydrated and mincing
girls just learning to dance in groups of three
the magic number associated with combs and wax
sanctuary of hives and desiccated tree-trunks
where hosts of malevolent spirits like ritual
undertakers pin the winds to the walls where
hundreds have already sacrificed their letters
to Her a hush of obscenities that split the seas
in half and rodent-like swarms underfoot and
the skies blackening with the hazy detrimental
sun whom Herself deformed midpoint lifting sistra
and soft drum-petals and incense wafted in slender
glass cylinders distant choirs of boy-brides drunk
by the age of eight and tottering between columns
of roseate sand sacked tills of dawn the archaic
syllabary meant to bring down the moon and
washed ashore the beautiful corpse of Adonis
whom none can touch oils and silt and magma
pouring through a secret funnel does *she* Shriek ?
the elevator and the rotunda and holy Acanthus
the Greeks can scarcely know Her the dozens
of shivered rock-hydras and hewn cedars littering
hill-slopes more ancient than thought a migration
of Mind and denizens of the *ideal* shaping
hand-sized porphyry dialects to shout ! *her*
becomes undone the marbles crushed by Israeli
tanks and what remains of her languishing speech
but homophones withering in the solar consonant
it is too much to ask of Catullus to upbraid her
disheveled and inconstant as ever was in her
boudoir of fake screens and fireflies the onyx
shape of her heart the bosom beating fast
a radiation of windows too remote to remember
black powders of eternity mushrooming silently
and night with its enormous palm fronds
descends with the tiny feet of galaxies
to separate her from her sleep
at last and alone

11-29-20

THE PASSING OF SAINT MAX

the time they put Angel on life-support
you could hear the windows rattling with traffic
unseen hosts dancing ions flagrant Brownian movement
the chaste both clean and impure the fossil thoughts
dragged into the fluorescent glare and x-rays
showing the descent of man from light and above
inches between the hospital roof and heaven a mad
rush of stars crushed in luncheon cellophane
how much was to weep and how much to destroy ?
could never recall exactly how the accident
or what month the day isolated itself and heat poured
through crevices in the ivy-strangled wall
Mozart's clarinet concerto played inside a tiny red suitcase
someone had neatly propped at the foot of the bed
nights came and went oblivious of the diurnal schedule
nights came to stay while distant rumors of water
and mountains beside themselves with envy or grief
one afternoon syntax and diagnosis just came apart
the charts went way off the diagram and needles
pointed to a red distance to a handcuffed planet
circling in a wild ellipse the *number* for eternity
a conjectured forty nine years that passed in a matter
of nanoseconds the future once immense with helium
went out hissing in a dizzy spiral when no one
was looking and hands became estranged and
the shapes of words lost all repercussion dissolving
in a hive of useless mantras no ear could decipher
sat there for days staring at the gauge that measures
just how far heat can go and the fusion of zeta
to its long-forgotten Egyptian house dark receptacle
of pharaohs and slaves alike difficult to maintain
composure bed-clothes stifling the shadow
small increments of memory turning to shale
and the luminous and numinous moment of splendor
known as *death* unplugged from the wall
and left to shift for itself beyond the turmoil
of scope and reason embraced Angel
like darkness caressing leaves at night

11-29-20

THE BURDEN OF MEMORY

next door to red is the consciousness of blue
the escape route to the stars is a stairway of smoke
the legions who tangle down below in an inferno
three inches long by one twice as thick
do you know what day it is today ? *Saint Mnemosyne's* !
there is no such thing as the hour before last
a blur of missing syllables a tonic of vocalic
justice but a defeat for the aphasia of knowledge
to understand a thing or two only brings grief
sorrow in the forbidden grass a prison house of dew
to learn to talk ! to swing on the paradise of thought !
a child two children count them all astray
why did we ever ? and recall the time a motor
was installed in the parlor and doors yanked open
and in come the shadows bearing damaged fruit
it' a mystery Troy was ever written !
a secret illness in the mouth a scabbard of lies
situations without reversal a labyrinth composed
only of solar consonants and the blackening of time
I remember this I remember that but *when* ?
the race to finish reading in order to win !
suddenly age is upon us solemnities of disorder
and mourning and corteges filing down the avenue
eight meters long and recitations of poetry
in languages yet to be deciphered a hand goes up
a revolution of fingers ! enumerate the leaves
as they turn their faces to the light listening
for the quiet repercussions of distance and water
alone as always to the last and knocking the knee
against the enormous wall of oblivion My Love !
books all over the place pages wide open
to texts of alarm and death the ministry of thunder
eviscerated vowels shapes of air summer winds
bearing the corpses of *nouns* deprived of sound
the once and for all of lexicons burdened with memory
etymologies and punctuations and stellar drift
the mind ! to wake ! yawning abyss of yesterday
the shoulder carrying forty thousand histories
libraries of alternate universes a jungle
of semiotic memorizations futility of all endeavor
the song you cannot get out of your head !
the song you cannot get out of your head !

11-30-20

SONNET : REPERCUSSION

the least first dread the sleep and loss
darkness as sweet as the unspoken hive
lingering such as lives can the thread frays
days are not equal words lose all shape
meanings have no sound the lesson is stray
junction of consonant and endeavor the fling
hands a spray to the girl in crimson mind
attitude and leaf sinking tomb of memory
the dried seas beside shadows of wind and
sand destruction is all nothing has duration
a file of discarded dust the power to drill
deep into rock and myths that endanger
simply by telling and what eye can resolve
distinctions of sky and night a repercussion

11-30-30

THE IMMATERIAL ADDICTION OF THE SELF
"a imaterial adição de si mesmo"
Clarice Lispector

syllable by syllable can we alter what was originally meant?
time is the hallucination and space the solid evidence
as we circumambulate with a Sanskrit intensity
and devotion the invisible planet that survives us
the demented weathers of the first hour continue
in their literal progress through the dawn's former
radiance the stuttering and starting horses that
pause as if having a thought before racing madly
through the restructured gateway of pure light
a hand is to discover as fingers are to lose
the day is a great project of forgetting the desert
from which we arise rejecting bed and simulation
of sleep and the registers in coppertone or helium
to recognize instead in one another denizens of
a previous life the very death of this one distributed
in sections of memory hemispheres of a forbidden
future or a cinema of disbelief will you not also abide
by the doorway and if addressed use the honorific
pronoun the great *Usted* that clarifies personal distance
mountains without horizons that force noon upon
the protagonists of this lunar play-act the fierce
summer storm visible with the third eye and dancing
molecules that represent Shiva in his destructive mode
shatters and shivers of a sea on its knees rolling
with an angry tide against the cities we so carefully
mapped on a strange July afternoon halting oranges
and crayon-bright crimsons for thoroughfares
or the realization that once outside the self we

can begin to be as we were and shades and nuances
of mind and the impermanence of all thoughts
a goddess appears with a suddenness of electricity
a discovery of myth and rejuvenation but only
for a minute before darkness the wild swirl of
emotions in love it seems and a thread needling
through the circular distinctions of the persona
I am that as you are also whom I never meant to be
seeing through the vowels and conjectures of
a psyche that is telling its own tale of obscurity
with sounds meant to resemble a vocabulary
of leaves and oblivion a finality to any day
that we cannot hang on to and sliding into a maze
dusky equivalent of conscience and a mentality
owned by the body and its shadowy repercussion
a harrowing and indistinct phantom language
which possesses us the statues deep within who
contract disorder and grief rehearsing oracular roles
and beautiful as the lines recited are of the poem
none there are who can translate it

12-01-30

SOME EXTRA SONNETS FOR THE COMING DARK

i

Juno the poisoned mice on the moon planet-husbands
tilled furrows of mythic disorder the world asunder
space cracks in half either hemisphere at a loss
for misery and bad punctuation I told you so
it wouldn't work out the illusions the increments of
azure at either end of sleep wind currents darkening
tying tree-tops into who knows the twins dividing
summer into bright and obscure the swimming pool
the deaths the highways the imminent fix of cities
falling into the lake asteroids and uranium and a film
loop showing interiors of pyramids and song-cycles
alone a loss at last a leaf in full aphasia and hands
that blot the secrets of time in a single career rash
and crimson ellipses stars shaking hair and Juno

ii

sad as the masters can be the grief of red and bleak
as air in its tubular cemetery who can avoid tears
the friction of mind against memory the vowels that
stand for each zodiacal mansion the Mexicans at
the crossroads in tattered and ankle-white the rose
turned into hemp and the daily bazooka stillness
of beads wrestling hands grass dense as evenings
in the acute hospital wards windows pitch-thick
a night balanced on its own pronoun so many the

sorrowing hills each tree a foster city dormant
with lull and drone of hives the branches that reach
sky-ward a height of furious ants the ledger with
numbers of no account backwards in stained glass
shoulders burdened with a catastrophe of dew

iii

miasma the corollary of sound that depths ken
as ancient becomes a puzzle between palaces the
erosion of water a specter of dynamite in the hair
sleeping which is an ear at a time and sheaves
of day-old wheat the goddess a lunatic in torn denim
who haunts the microwave a fixture of eyes gleam
haunting the empty pastures why it cannot be at
the back of space the rolling crescent of heat aglow
grammar at a standstill between two archaic noises
and a shift to glean through parsimony of thought
the mind's brief accident bearing on traffic a mute
and solemn dirigible crashing in the inch of a cymbal
who is not his brother's dappled keeper clouds that
orient the future of death with a small blank leaf

iv

granular reconstruction of the sun *Ace of Spades*
great black wingless moth dayflight of nocturnal
arabesques its chase is over its Pegasus long dead
reversal of all constellations the half of breath
souls cling to before their departure a shaft of
rays fossil centipedes leaving signatures in the sky
absences too many to number first loves first deaths
philosophies of renunciation a god is sleeping shh!
anguish desire and insect reunions govern his dream
though we are always in the midst there is no center
bracken weeds algae of illusion tides breaking stone
words ! husks and variations of a *single* sound drone
of light hemisphere of memory dovetailed hands
dissolving in the hills among dark shapeless leaves

12-02-20

EMPTY DAYS : **MAX** *IN ABSENTIA*

the surgeon and coroner play solitaire with left hands
words are only unuttered breaths the sentiment
that *all* is only part of the half we should realize
before the hour is up conjecture of a mythic sunset
mire and morass of thought wrapped and put
into a storage box and futility of endeavor silence
best expressed with vowels borrowed from a liturgy
religious exercises in the tumulus and a brief
association with light whatever else matters is
small comfort to the survivors whose senses remain
the property of a flawed deity a smoking height
a distance of compounded grief and hills evaporating
in the window's ominous reflections come nightfall
to think that his breath straddled two *centuries !*
memories when he was OK nine years old pedaling
his bike to Brooklyn Heights and back and silly
games and tiny sounds of syllables and allocations
of sudden happiness and ropes of rhyme and air
such it was when archaic rock and sediment
turned to blank quarters of an inchoate dream
unimaginable hues resonances *disorder* of space
this day these days this era of disease and manipulation
headlines full of catastrophic ciphers and delusions
freight trains stuck in glacial seasons without reprieve
a hundred thousand seconds counted backwards
between a pair of unnamed avenues and lock-downs
what's to live for what's the gain in salvation ?
there are no numbers greater or less than *Three* !
knowledge is a discarded brick and information a lie
the almighty Zeus of epic a lingering smoke in doubt
what's come and gone and been translated is a hoax
sheets out to dry the past is in the missing sky
to grieve and mourn to fix the mind in old re-runs
to rearrange the furniture and knit new crosswords
asleep in a distance which is already here
look to the grass that hasn't grown for years
search the concrete in front for a solitary silhouette
memory is a repercussion between deaf ears like
the glint of sea in the mortician's eye an echo of salt
unplayed games doors without knobs speechless leaves
and *Max* a shadow on the wall when no one's looking

12-02-20

ORPHEUS : THE RECOGNITIONS

gnomic stance of the hero at the gate when of a
sudden catastrophe like a fling of rabid flies
green span of envy and dross the rapture of gods
whose only motive is to destroy through oracular
deceits bringing down a thunder of moons and
whiplash of circular threats planet after planet
smoking out of alignment the haze of despair
paramount disorder of the unities and a blaze
of macron and circumflex lighting the back brain
for a brief eternity called life on earth a speechless
statue yearning for mortality and the dozens of
sailors deceived by promises of golden hives and hills
no wont of plenty and daughters-of-the-sun intrepid
in their palaces of haunted marble such as it is !
myth the splendor of cloaks woven by Aphrodite
only to wake face down drugged in the mire of
an apocalypse re-living an incident from a former life
thin silhouette of light shimmering ache of a fruit
rotting in the hand by noon and fulminated by
the *recognitions* the ignition of mind and its self
darkness of the sea and the metaphors of survival
afar the lands and more distant yet the mountains
of sound and clutter of repercussions and echoes
poetry reorganized by vowel and euphony afloat
in the derelict ear of the eternal adolescent *Orpheus*

12-03-20

THE GOD OF WEDNESDAYS

with incensed mind are born the unknown
raised and with fists the heralds scour the distances
where a mountain could be the ancient edge of light
and to the fray ignorant that fate has cut the thread
already and the seas with their awash and sands roiling
underneath a wonder that is to begin the second hour
poorly of syntax endowed the pectorals and incisions
made overnight the dwindling flesh to remain ever
but failing then dropping into dust the shields
interpolating as it were letters adapted to sounds
not found in the brain and to relax the hold and
free let the spirit soar unseen the sight brooding
of clouds and hardware of the skies drifting
moorings in the dense opacity where thought
no longer matters piercing the lobe to insert
magnificent the polished stone on its inkling
and on the other side of rain where each ekes
a life at the end hands prayer lifted by the altar
unfinished as words often are to the goddess in raiment

dazzling of archaic white the verses borrowed from a
Canopic source the legend in glyphs hortatory as twins
are and can be the following adjective the sorted
lots parks and pottery glazed red with attributes
how could they end so briefly the quick notation
of breath and luminous specters the falling from
heaven and landing thud on metal carapaces to be
buried in lime and asbestos the soldered parts
no longer resemble the body as such and looming
larger than writ allows the *God-of-Wednesdays* knocking
at the hospital gate haunted expression his winged cap
and sandals fleet as ever bearing messages of the dead
and harbinger of lost seasons of storm and truss
it was inevitable *I am so sorry for your loss*
glyphs and orientations the immense moon of memory
are these the rocks that sing ? river that runs backwards
a loss of leaves the trees obedient to the winds
everything shaking infinitely and without sound
the substitute for bread is sorrow

12-04-20

THE HYMN TO JUNO

leaps from the ether in ire goddess Juno
whom before tremble in fear the denizens
of this or that peninsula their forbears had
a sin committed an offering omitted in blaze
the thickened smoke rising lest they appease
wrongly and yet do flare their countenances
for which read of death the first signs writ
big and hap they confound mind and illusion
even to this day as doth she foment and rage
trestles crossing and iron smelted in her glare
do smaller beings melt away and insect heights
a domain of under-foot and wrath roaring
flames to the hills flee weary woken from sleep
the soft den the cubicles of grassy lair a keep
from the shoals and unerring fixes her aim
helped by lordly beloved of her Alcides his cult
in the gymnasium and rout loud the consonants
from oracle and prayer and sought then to end
mortal sway over such and such a realm as found
in books the bosky splendor and dusk declines
day's smitten hour a hill erects with bristling
conifer and brims over with repercussions swell
punctuating this brief devastation with verses
lofty but unheard their splendor the echo of
caves the ware and bracken that toils the ear
a leafy token of impaired beauty the glistening
and sweat shines the skin of her the Queen

whom on either throne as sister or wife
proclaims the dense tragedy of origins obscure
as worlds come to wrestle worlds and cosmos
imperil with eternal strife the mind's function
and words dispel anointing sounds with loss
of meaning the running loose of syllables
quickened by their lack of shape and sense
and to sleep return the hand that once spoke

12-04-20

THE SPECTACULAR MOMENT OF COMING AND GOING

to speculate is to enervate the lives and people
the masks you've worn the thoughts that drained
you midnights in tow with the forbidden goddess
dreamer and spoke of a wheel duration of time
for three minutes only afternoons in a Sunday of
red wine and marijuana cigarettes some kind of
Mexican apotheosis waiting over there in a motel
dedicated to *Chac Mool* and the rains keep coming
down and the spray painting on the stucco wall
never dries depicting the volcano and its aftermath
gardens of daunting euphoria trees and hummocks
and the wild but tiny voice of *Hylas* being dragged
under by the Nymph could have been you as well
out on a lark testing the limits of jazz inside a cracked
horn solo packing and unpacking the same suitcase
on a rooftop in an imitation Paris where the ghost
of Toulouse-Lautrec was your broken-legged guide
through the mansion of Bad Art which you embraced
tacking to the ceiling the superannuated nudes of
an ancient Mayan colony and watching the spirals
of their dancing legs the tom-toms of their gorgeous
velvet drum-heads spurs and spears and mountains
dominated by Mother-of-the-Gods who enticed you
and led you down Under to the whirlpools where
eyes of demons did their hypnotic act displaying
in a buzz and whir your past and previous births
spatial odyssey in liana and crimson ivy nooses and
one by one the exits wore out until this last one
with its rearing argent faces and moon-like drowsy
gaze brought you right back to the living room
of the house you dwelt in creating maps and schemes
copied from a *being* who could be none other than
the soft and talking leaf summoning you to sleep
forevermore in the windowless pyramid of the mind
cosmic illusion of the million and a half uncounted cells
biology and nadir of all-Presences *unimaginable*
as is your absence in the Toltec tattoo of time

12-05-20

AN ACCOUNT OF OUR AFTERNOON
AT POINT REYES DURING COVID

was closed to us the Vedanta Park and
scattered the holy white and tiny deer
a sense was the end of all things visible
and material a sky lowering its daft cloud
-work a supreme being could not have done
better nor any of the bi-polar deities who
govern the ransacking of mortal thought
and mind so caught in the hiatus that curtails
movement and circling slowly the self-same
eddying pool now grown muddy with despair
we eked our way into an evening slit of wan
crepuscular glare the lamps on the oncoming
carts the horses charged to their creaking wains
gave little doubt the way was lost the error
to remain unchecked our past was curbed
by this new morass the present but a slender
epitome of darkness and the future forever
blocked to hand and eye and thus the metaphors
the similes of deluded breath the irony of air
receding from its enormous atmospheric base
and of us puny consciousness at odds with time
the minutes discounted the apostrophes and dots
heckling the skies with threatening asterisks
no road they showed no display of warnings
but a semiotics of disorder the grief of coming
to terms with who we really are the least of names
somber and sometimes witless shades clinging
to some shred of memory of the shapes of things
or vast echoes that tremble in the sleeping ear
but for all of that the freeway's hidden roar
the spirit of a broken mountain the wanton
destruction of the Ohlone path small sparks
and figments flying toward a swallowed sun
how bleak and black the vestry by the side
or the slanted tombstone on its wet tumulus
no direction led us to the fallen gate the door-
way to the sorrow that finally awaited us
the hour we never left the dormer and closet
shrouded in the events of that archaic moment
when universe and particular dissolve in one
brief and eternal sob

12-05-20

LA MUERTE DE ENRIQUE ARGÜELLES (12-05-1994)
para mi hermana Laurita

does it matter ? solitude and darkness the stifled
air the impatient concourse of atmospheres
dilated suns traversing the black stretch of woods
behind the mind's lonely reach to identify and
name to impersonate and copy the paintings and
sketches left undone by some artist's hand come
the last moment and the questions remain
unanswered the photos grainy with time dissolve
in an imperfect twilight of cloud and moon-rise
hills cluster before the thunder and expectations
of snow and improvisations of poetry but with
what words ! a noise issues from the descent of man
into the Stygian shoals syllables of shattered sounds
oracular debates in the depths of the ear a faint
repercussion of light gleaming disposals of memory
why is that a way to be ? a series of montages and
delayed stage effects persons dropping their masks
falling in free flight from the podium of birth
the annex of emotions and the slow dissolution of
recognitions inarticulate shapes moving to and fro
and a lector bearing reeds and broken branches
announces something to the doorman who stands
holding a glass representation without knowing what
or why the end has come as to so many others
and turns from the fray of possibilities the mirror
offers to address the now unrecognized soul
departing the room if only consciousness and heat
could sustain this ineffable moment while a
kaleidoscopic train of images takes him far back
to the sun-washed rooftops of Guadalajara a lone
and inkling infancy separating light from light

12-06-20

THE BOOK OF LIBERATION

one dies we all die the weather report stays the same
in Greek it's a unilateral decision to war with Troy
while others may have diphthongs to declare at customs
prepared to board the boat of deceptions and sail away
here it's the reign of sorrow and mountains and tiny
glyphs orienting hair and ribbons of Naiads lurking
in the brush for who can say which will be the hour
when they cry *Time's up !* and the host of illusions
that bore us to the fray scatter like brittle leaves
in the ever *triste* autumn winds isn't it just the way
the rishis told us and to follow the speckled peacock
into the unmapped woods to surrender this and that
gift or arm or even the grip of thoughts that hold
us hostage to the ego a maypole of flurry and buzz
the swarms of winter bees blindly colliding in sleep
with the tangle of histories elaborated on the backside
of rivers sparkling madly towards the Sea-of-Being
and dawn springs on us between pages of written and
unwritten codes and poems and sketches of an idea
about just who we thought to be passing through a glass
reversing all indications of birth and death icons half-
measured for their weight in time and slowly dissolving
the *yes* of our beings shadow-forms reluctant to surrender
consistency and matter yet we do lose hold everything
starts to slip away the constellations that scoured
the eye the canyons and rushing shores the ear contained
the loves and more that crazed us for a week or two
vowels and pigments and dulcet tones a vibrato lifted
into the atmospheres singing the broken promises made
between furrows of summer corn to love forever and a day
shattered the mirror held upside down the combs and
ointments the face-lift and bronzing tans to prolong
youth ! yoga and lip-balm the messages of the munis
whose memory consists of the *Book of Liberation*
peace and shanti-Om and the consonants that linger
before emptying the mind of all noise and wholesale
editions of the texts of oblivion and the contours of words
gone from the speech of statues and us and you and them
all in between the asterisks that gyrate around the head
rock-fragments vows of silence dissolution of atoms
what the body knows is but a ring of water returning
to the clouds vapors and unnamed essences all that
vanishes in the vast impermanence of space

12-07-20

THE ORACULAR MOMENT

and having crossed the sea approaching now
the craggy shoreline beware the route to the left
descending for it takes you to Hades
and you will hear the rushing Acheron just
feet away but blindfolded by memory you will
mistake this for the snowy ravine behind the
garden plot and think to traverse it by
light of day but confusion and darkness will
hold sway the trembling maps the meters
separating you from the hell-chasm illusory
neither will you be able to return over the small
ravine to till the garden plot nor will memory
serve you as to who you are in defiance of
the will of the gods and on your right will
appear many mountains misty steep and dark
as in a painting with waterfalls and trees slanting
sidewise jutting into the impermeable airs
at this point nothing avails and you will trust
only to a copy of memory to the slight repercussions
in the ear to the wavering tensions of light
and into a dream-state falling you will
among statues awake again and hear the roaring
syllables of a mantic voice or the bellows of
Hephaistos inventing ingenious devices horses
armor stately palaces et cetera you will remain
benighted plunged into this or that crevice
of time and assume new identities recalling
nothing of what went before and pursue
in this oblivion new loves and careers claiming
a part of the sky as your own ! then will come
crashing the bottoms of heaven the tempests
of mind and thought swirl of insects with human
faces and between two lives past and present
and shield and spear to dust turn and falling
face down in the spongy turf your brains
will be excited with the riots of a false salvation
how many deities smoking a single cigarette will
perch on the small branch of anthropology inches
above your stray heads and proclaim your losses
how does one depart from this labyrinth ?
bewilderment and identity !
the noose of consciousness ! where is the small
garden plot now the one you tilled every spring
and mayflies and blossoms and trill of jays
a morning in forever ! gone !
asleep in an improvised story-book bed
none of this will come back to you and devoured
by the insistence of night you will dissolve again
into the small and shaking leaves
lingering by the dark garden wall

                                12-07-20

THE HOLLOWS

it's that end of life feeling , you know
you've reached the 5th Book of the Iliad
, somehow can't turn the next page to see
just whom Apollo is slaying between which
apostrophes, end of life sensation the afternoon
doldrums , see the dun hills moving dusk , hear
the catastrophe in the well , a surgeon making
decisions where to cut the hour in half what ,
moving slowly through planetary shifts and
paradigms , end of life , seize the hand before
it immobilizes , the theft of liturgies and
having to sit on hard wooden pews listening
to the bombast of a white-frocked , was what
the bard intended to convey the thrill of
a shore moving out to sea , or the husk of
night settling on the shattered camp site ,
horses of strategic nobility shot through the
crupper aghast the oracle , plain-chant
drilling the ear the monotony of hives , dormant
sounds nascent echoes deathly hush eloquence
of what cannot be said sitting for all , eternity ,
the great unfinished poem ushered in by
quotation marks and small red dots and the
leaven of bread baked on the corner , where
and why , who and how the versions replicate
and resonate and whisper and drown , a
brother standing alone below the cliff of anti-
cipation and doubt , a brother moving forward
on feet borrowed from the tutelary deity of
unreason , the end of matter ! tiny cycles of
paper heavens burning just below the line
that separates gravity from weight , background
of asterisks and exclamation marks , questions
and profound incisions in the earlobe where to hang
the famous crystal chandeliers of Juno , it
is the tenth birthday of everybody and girls
named for the thousand clouds of infinity sing
their hit-parade of number one songs , cakes blow
up !!! mother in her sick-room gown floral pattern
and starched looms over it all , comb and brush
and pallor that can only mean death , cemetery and
sanitarium what's the difference , calling home
between and through the tombstones , names
come and go aflutter in late afternoon deep ,
darkened , the remains , someone surrenders his
hands to the police , postscript and lottery
in the small wooden church at the end of time ,
song birds and Bach organ recitals , gloaming
and somber , forced to sit there during
the sermon describing hell much like
the basement with the furnace going night ,
and day , the hollows in the pit of the stomach ,
how to go home and sleep after that , ? ,

12-08-20

APOLLO OF THE DAWN

to hymn the remnants mountain-tops a glisten
folded inwards the night's scalpel and blades
releasing stars from their bright and Lo !
descending from some hidden height his toxic
bow a quiver with argent sheen his unkempt
locks with dew moistened over his cheeks unfurled
deity of Light Apollo chrome-plated and of
song the hero eyes darting ruthlessly across mortal
terrain while even as altars are set up the swift roe
slain for sacrifice and question men in their sleep
do we wake to celebrate or die ? does the number
three not suffice and what of Mopsus and Orpheus
their descant and syllabic detail ? long run
the roads to nowhere and sea and dry-land alike
merciless in their spite towards mortals and what of
the uncounted who went before by Fate smitten
stupidly in last week's oriental battle and incense
and burning fat to the heavens spiral odors a
surmise that all can be fixed that salvation
is an inch away from the throw of spit the poisoned
allergies that plague nor the formidable moment
no longer postponed when breath is halved and
then totally removed yet slowly and with the weight
of secret ores does the god move with his panoply
of lamps and intimate blazes over the topographies
of an archaic atlas and with deft hand sheers human minds
of their error moving ever straight to the slopes
dried brush and thistle covered the approach to
Olympus with its summer weathers and disdain
all history pivots in his thimble and the future
of progress but a poor reflection in a shop window
then in his careless passage each step making earth
tremble and the waters to seize in a terrific aphasia
hover as shadows in dubious throes the souls
of earthly travelers dumbfounded and shipwrecked
the crew of the Argo dazzled and bedimmed at the
new day's marvelous origins ere darkness hold sway

again

12-09-20

SYMPLEGADES : SONNET

what with waves and rocks like the swelling horns
of bulls yoked to sweat the goddesses nimble-footed
leaping fogs roaring and the clashing horses of spume
and dust dissolving in the eye's choleric mists a hill
moves more rapidly than the steer swift and vague
a voice without vowels and heights within the brim
of a chase between timbers from mountains hewn
alike the noon and its shadow dappled in the small
hour of everlasting day torment and sputum hilt
and chaser whitening the dark stripe of life and
stricken skies lower with fortune's coerced self
a copy of clouds mapping destiny and futility the
same as ever was in beautiful gushes of horrific
sea-thrusts the cliffs clangor with stupefied lyrics

12-09-20

THREE SONNETS : THE DARK SPELL

a

like thoughts without words little clouds
issue from my head into the vast enormity of air
labyrinth and memory of sleep in the archaic sands
would ever these small and soundless is it
the spirit that moves us the decline rotating
and heavens like broken wheels out of joint
spinning my head these little fogs clots of noise
the recording device shot loops running round
and round the oblique turf of dreams and they
are dead the mourned and missing pages the
lacking all evidence did they exist a question
full of marks and caesuras and the illogic
of the misplaced hiatus the forbidden vowels
in the speech of statues spliced and deviated

b

focus of language in each leaf the torn tongue
sounding illusory memories the stint on the moon
peregrinations to Jerusalem the mocked stone a-
float in the waters of unreason repercussion and echo
in the hand the mutilations of space between inches
separating the spear-head from its target the heart
of the epic each horse an epitome of dust rearing on
its hind quarters just as twilight with its waves of
bleak and nausea setting off to sea storm wilderness
even as the waxen consonants of the sun dissolve
in that improbable noon inside the Sybil's bottle
green as envy the tusks of desire the infatuation

overload and schism of mind SOS to the zeta
that sustains and the rushing grasses of oblivion

c

and finally it says under the perforated thought no
words can bring no amount of grief the unlimited
sorrow of echo at the border of water and function
heights and broad causes in the reeds where ink
dries swifter than Fate's nod the atavistic dream
of syllables I am having as dawn erupts the light
polyphony of lamps and oil the incision in the head
all holy the winnowing of memory rock formation
and brooding the limitless holding back but fails
the tears that ruin and which is the shape that
becomes a hand and which that is only a phrase
in a botched Greek text about the *nous* does misery
generate resonance ? asks the purloined deity
mouths flames anchors stems darkness the all

12-10-20

DECEMBER ELEGY 2020

breath of blood the thumb a leaf encounters
life-time shadow marvel shrouded without edge
sequences in rock and storm of distant water
each side of the rain in perpetuity the smallest
vowel the inch of space beneath the worm a
legend of lawns and sprinklers and bodies
caved in by automatic spokes the wheel of talk
the speechless cadaver statues brought to light
a warning to the sun blackening in its homophone
the awful distinctness of the *other* immobile as
the fraction of fire the insistence to dream awake
fossil and circumflex above the mistaken sound
when did echo ever reach this far asleep in stone
the tongue without noise the dirge and catastrophe
a friction of stories innate repercussion of mind
waking suggestions of anomie so beckon here
the finger's index a judgment of hands seeking
retribution for their loss of shape recollection
of grass mounted behind glass a face at a time
the single ones gone ! mine him was the one so
small on his feet leaping like a cricket on the vine
and they gather sheaves of wheat and iron collars
to spare the night its white spray and prayers
they offer to a god of humiliation a Sanskrit moon
sandalwood lifting in the overheated dark swift
the unseen bird of thought gone mad and flames
a schism of mantras darkening the empty spot
we used to live here this craggy sump this earth

a device brought us down and leaves still shaking
the torment of salt and flashes of ire the hills
endow as sinking the west implores its steeds
but none return the graven pitch of sorrow

12-10-20

THIS SMALL BELOVED SIMPLE HAND
> *"però les mans, ja cendra*
> *o llum, on retrobar-les?"*
> Salvador Espriu

whose skull doesn't grow dusk with memories
the gilded darkness of the sun emitting solos
for horn and lost statue and lips seasoned with
silence in a marble grove attest to the funereal
abracadabra of heroes paraded like shadows
on the thoroughfare of loss last winter the seams
and terrors of water seemed too near now grief
no less old mounts its ashen wave higher into the night
alone and sorrowing the rock where buried voices
tangle with distance for accord between the sutures
wounds of hands and fingers missing in the grass
of an evening without summer and even if tears can
bring eyes back the light is a record of futility a
verger absent from the myth of Persephone the fragile
humus beneath her feet and the tug of her mother's
arm as the boxed sky of eternity inches across hills
far to the west of gravity a lone leaf a fragment of
verdure the weeping deep within the ear whose
traps of bird-song and flight are a dolorous reminder
of childhoods left unfinished in the archaic sand

12-11-20

THE DEPARTURE

for once the missing dactyls and spondees
relieve us of the day's diminishment the hours
allotted to the despairing mind the smallest
sequence of stars making appearance at noon
the milestones suffering the repeated grief
we cannot escape their tom-tom's solemn drill
sadness and rain the usual symbols at the glass
the reverse of which is the long eternity
we must traverse before becoming light again

words were they no more than indistinct sounds in echo
like the waters of repercussion receding into sleep's
unknown bower the shapes and elisions of something
imperfectly remembered and when it comes to surface
the months that cannot be distinguished the beds
and lairs and myths of forged realities we call life
all at a distance and submerged in the constellations
flickering at the tip of a telescope do we then recall
why it was we lay as if hypnotized on summer grass ?

phonetic deterioration of the mind aphasia and ether
putting us out on the long table trying to read the
small print in the surgeon's eyes the gassy sound
of speech coming out of the mouths of statues draped
in the albescent shrouds of memory the suddenness
of rocks in the middle of the road or a chasm where
knowledge disappears darkening the contours of thought
edges of water lichen and moss and trophies of bark
ancient indications of distance and the loss of gravity

the poet's body the lessening vowels the circumflex
and archaic quotation of hands restless to have back
their memory of shape and clouds scudding into the eye's
deep anterior the speech of rock and blossom the dark
of the leaf torn from its voice the ethereal spirals and
projections of breath just when it coincides with air
the consonants of dissolution the knees and where
they go and numbness of the shoulders departing
as they turn into the soul's invisible soundless wings

12-11-20

ADOLESCENCE : THE LOST SEASON

to flee and not remember those days
the golden wheat in rows as summer
lost its glow declining in hills of a stupefied ore
the lesson of jingo and rattle the verb systems
pronounced dead before arrival stone and concrete
the heights of a single finger against the crushing
envelope of atmospheres a cloud without rain
spearheaded by lonesome cries from beyond
a snapshot of time before it accelerated
standing outside the drug-store window scattered
with elocution and demand for a lower step
angels in mufti looking exactly like the homecoming
princesses or copies of the nymphs who stole books
from the library and to adore trees ! and the small
fictions of the telephone and bus-stop waiting
for the mind to photograph its sweetheart
pinafore and hair in adjacent ivory combs
the gift of Venus ! songs without melodies
and the reasons for words lost in the fray
what a noise to live ! sections of air and winter
snowstorms grey deposits oblivion falling
softly throughout the unending December night
when an hour took two months to finish
and Lo waking to the nuisance of star-fade
days becoming the labyrinth of education and
the tunnel that leads one-way to death
hold my hand ! forever a syllable and a wish
and seven decades later in the uniform
of a retired civil servant wasted and longing
what is there to hold dear ? the lawns !
the single peculiar moment shining like
a precious metal lost in the capsized stream
running backwards through the dance of memory
fugitive on loan from the gods ! repercussion !

12-12-20

ANOTHER YEAR PASSING DARK

leaving the dark source of water
the lake slowly approaches the light
night ! abysmal memories of flame
the edges of the inch of space we live
the woods naked and stark their labyrinth
the snake that looks for its own trace
our breath the cold figment of air descends
nor to the north where small reflections
glimmer on the surface reminders of the
faces that own us the descriptions of stars
dead we seem to be the clarity of gold
aging in our missing hands the ankle-
deep mire the moors of a spent winter
ourselves the dense thought of sounds
trapped in their cells of mind ancient
as the grass receding in the lambent dew
would dawn return its swart steeds
the question palms up toward the sun
of hesitating syllables rising in the black
nocturnal ends the fiction of some yesterday
a whitening tassel embroidered around
the eye the simple distance of a leaf
shaking in its aphasia the winds and
gusts diplomas of a remote lamp
the hills a ruin of vowels and noise where
once feet took us to gaze solemnly at our
own persons by the lake enduring dark
the longing unexpressed for lives
unspoken the trees that yearn for sky

12-12-20

DAZE : THE STORY OF MEDEA

multiple cores the evolution of water germinating
in pure sun bright the anxious arrival of quadrupeds
and more clambering over rock and reef to higher ground
you know the story well and the fuse of consciousness
and the armor and gadfly and the bite of truth
blood shadowing stone in a novelty of epic when
brother against brother and the gain of letters
and systems to record and erase and the panoply
of thoughts about this that and the everything
star-gazers and initiators of technique and drill
the fundament of reason in unreason and days
numbered like streets for their unexplained progress
today is no better when it comes to understanding
the root of our daze the fictionalized content of mind
the unfurling sails of an interminable voyage across
the Sea-of-Being narcolepsy and aphasia and *manicomio*
and the Lord of Death waiting in the alleyways and
each of us assigned a cipher a figment of identity
a suit of cards without rules to play the game and when
love walks in the side door and a screen of fireflies
and clusters of words entangled abused sounds a noise
like swarms of bees trying to make sense or is it
better to remain as statues incompletely informed
of the surrounding light and the activity of speech
then does music dun the head a wild improvisation
of jazz horns and drum-skins made from wild deer
to make an issue of things to make matter enduring
a daze in as many months to conclude the idyll of breath
and which of us is ever sure the lapel is straight
or that the mirror itself is a copy of something else
we cannot quite remember but for the lyric of pollen
and clouds and the noise we call poetry do we come
to terms that comprehension is out of the question
night finds us dusky presences pointillistic references
to events that occurred the day before yesterday
a space in which to recover for a moment only from
the fall and then ether sets in with its globes of oblivion
the long siege of unconsciousness the daze without end
her cheeks at first yellow turned blush red when first she laid
eyes on Jason and Eros muffled in the heat of noon
took instant flight leaving the maids in a state of amaze

12-13-20

A KIND OF LOVE POEM

what word is not without ambiguity
sequence of sounds rattle and gourd
of sleep nuisance of disconnected syllables
the talk between statues in unguarded hours
when nothing particular is ever meant
when a dream bears its noise into daylight
the puzzled mind the finger that forgets
the small elocution lost in the rushing grass
what single vowel remains intact in
the insect's ear the mumbled gravel
outside the window when night descends
strings of consonants that by three PM
are buried by schoolboys in hermetic Latin chalk
no energy inheres to the vaulted circumflex
and but slight movement on the edge of OM
mantras that cause leaves to shake and
mysterious effect of the solar homophone
when noon will not leave its shift
and consider the misinterpreted hieroglyphs
that lie entranced on the rock's wet border
what dead pharaoh can culminate in their score
no eye to scan or read the Sybil's chant
the volume of decibels that reach the moon
remains unrecorded in the x-rays of desire
what parenthetical remark what iota subscript
what ergative construction can pacify the verb
the stillness of the unwritten page like
water in its repercussive silence announces
for once the hiatus of the unexpressed thought
as a poem written without vocables
to be sung by unhewn marble figurines
who share the balance of time with caryatids
and when this love lyric reaches you
saturated in hexameters of an unseen lake
you too will be negated an omicron adrift
in the missing hemispheres of space

12-13-20

"AS I LAY DYING"

modulations of grief the rest of a lifetime
each with its own dialect beyond the written standard
lengths of shadow that seem to sever the moonlight
sounds crepuscular and nebulous clouds of echo
passing from this life to the next in hidden waves
a voice among the leaves a hand with its own subject
begins the incomplete and indistinct phrase a statue
perhaps or the indentation of dormant marble
sorrow intensifies its unspoken syllables deep within
the nocturnal heart a distance of no more than three
yards across the lawn of sleeping grass swept
by dreams fingers have longing to be connected again
switches of air tablets of wind designs of anterior skies
the size of spreading ink with even less clarity
mourning and its asbestos of indecision weeping
against an irreversible glass with repercussions of mercury
fatal incisions in hair the ear in respite of what it
needs to forget seas of monotonous repetitions mounting
a stairway just behind the lattice of smoke and memory
the perhaps of forbidden conjunctions in vertigo
just as the walls behind water seem to waver becoming
more distant like hills of an immobile color and
the entire structure of night collapsible and loud
comes apart in the window of human error and longing
noises of insects rumors of an epic language and tarot
symbols and shields asterisks and verbatim clauses
reported among the fading stars no greater than dew
receding from the eye's brief history of light

12-14-20

IN THE ABSENCE OF MEMORY

survival in the log-jam of words mere sounds
temptation to emerge as pure breath a round
of wind and glass distances possible only in sleep
the infirm sense of waking when dawn is still
captive in its monogram of silence aging yet
as we are an exchange of hands and weather
rustling in the leaves a suppressed rage to become
other once again a stain on the atmosphere a
voice without syllables a performance for the eye
resembling as all acts do a finality to things a
reckless information of mind a subject without
object and on and on as if salvation were possible
if there are latitudes behind the firmament
where gravity and time have no effect and
dreaming it is so both past and present the *child*
within the microscopic emotions in demand of
a speech to express them and a ruin of mountains
waters and mists painted in the back-brain as if
to remember ! *something* but what a playground
a street with no access a city beneath the lake
the future is no longer possible ! fingers reject
knives and ears hesitate before echoing clouds
among the hollyhocks and marigolds a Lazarus
dazed looks for his shadow and suddenly a phone
begins its dial tone and the immense air gathers
its copies of memory and dew and whatever
comes afterwards and the culmination of grass
even as twilight descends on its horses of dust
and a woman the shape of *paradise* merges
soundlessly into the great enigmas of night

12-14-20

AN ELEGY FOR MAX

of what use is the universe
    gas and protons and nebulae ?
what matter the outer ramparts of fire
    the lessening of space the blow-up
at start and finish the burning winds
    a thousand isolated galaxies
the small and feckless worlds of seeds
    anemones and blow-warts and
seizures of the sun in its homophone
    is black the reverse of speed
and by the dozens do dead infants wail ?
    alas alone the leaf inside the poet's
mind the thoughts that blaze and smoke
    the waters in their eternal repercussion

echo and tight-rope and imbalance of the brain
        night-skies spackled with violent asterisks
the charm of hexameters hewn from rock
        sandy explosions of the sea at birth
how does the vacuum work within
        unintended rhyme and why does
porphyry form a statue all on its own
        exactly who is the second one
from the right in the class photograph
        or the disappeared face in the mirror
when dawn strikes its hoof on the anvil
        which of the twenty moons
will Medea bring down first in love
        and why should the grizzled Boatman
ask for a fare to pass into oblivion ?
        what are the protocols of quanta
and which of the three thousand and one deities
        is the one to pray for salvation ?
asteroids hominids grappling-hooks of thought
        Cyclopean citadels in dreams undone
black-holes and the Ramayana in ballet
        the verb *to know* is not the same as *to be*
nor does memory have any value buried
        in the encyclopedia of heat
which world to choose and revile
        which cosmos to set ablaze
which death must be endured to understand
        the randomness of breath
"leave me alone I want to die
        a leaf in the eternal light !"
there is no egress nor hypothesis of longing
        ellipses and eclipses and angels
that come and go in the eye's small breadth
        the rope of fallibility
the chasm and the inch of hell
        the famous weathers of infinity
when consciousness strikes its brass
        resolution of sound without words
syllables of unreason vowels scattered
        among consonants of unknowing
what does not come back what can never be
        again my frail young son *Max*

12-15-20

THE GREAT DAY OF ANTIQUITY

the sun in its receding parenthesis and waters !
violent culmination of origins and flux of skies
enormous tragedies when cloud encounters cloud
I am a symposium of different others ! cries
the inarticulate god who covets mortality
and freezing weathers in the globe of sleep and
rains of silence pouring over the ghastly plain
where dead heroes look for their heads amidst
rust and the opprobrium of political lies
in this entr'acte of causality and pathos the flags
utter their fealty to the former air that circles
human destiny a pitiful handful of vowels and
the resignation of the circumflex and the iota
it comes and goes ! the eye is never secure
and the ear in its stone of unheard echoes
weeps at the margins of a stealthy darkness
how do we come to be ? it is the orient of women
the immense drama of clothing and cosmetics
strategies of the small box of poisons and lavender
there are curtains called heaven and backdrops
where rustic actors ululate at the midday moon
manicomio lunacy bedrock of beautiful illusion
by day's end the emptied amphitheater of thought
darkens forever more the footfalls and small
junctions of syllable and tone the unspeakable
statuary of the mind at a standstill haunted hills
distances of ink and plasma scrawled signatures
of deities who never learned to speak the vast
and impregnable fortress of space and longing
at the root of perpetual grief poetry of the hiatus
copies of mirrors blackened by the setting sun

12-16-20

CICADA
after Anacreon

your long day of grass
clinging to a single blade of light
you sing plunging your shrill note
through the green leaf of time
waters listen to your ear
your empire sheaves of wheat
shaking minutely in an air
that turns to dusky pallor
so far away from the ancient sun
pillar of sound and longing !
how dense is the minute
that seems to rival speed
how light the immense dark
that removes you from the day

12-16-20

JASON AND MEDEA

why chafe against destiny ?
the fates have already wed our names to the sand
come midnight next when tomorrow
is no longer a possibility and an ominous rook
with Hera's voice makes dulcet song a thrill
in the ears of those already plunged into darkness
how is it *dumbfounded in ethereal silence* a poetry
brings our homophones together and though not chaste
our hearts double the vowel that blends them
do we over-arch our desires distilling a secret botany
into our veins compelled by headstrong Aphrodite
how white the steps we take as if backwards
into the consonants that undo meter and LO
the process of night weaving and tangling
thread and beam in the opprobrium of breath
come be my sweet and last forever in my swells
rush the ebb and flow of our mouths and seal
the hour's only exit as to doom fated our grief and timing
escape the event's minute clockwork a draft
of love and an outsize portfolio of ink where
promises elide and are diluted in a Greek pentagram
the bonzes of Alexandria in their library-maze
catalog our brief reunion and dolorous cries arise
from the Nile's seven mouths but here clasp
to my bosom the remains of your madness
infanticide and angel and the lunatic masonry of your
words a finality to reason and the brooding dawn
that will never come and rush the grasses and small
insects who carve empires in their soils and LO
again Hecate's nave the boudoir of our illusion

the nocturnal shrills and winged invisibilities
the terror unspoken in the brazen hoofed flames
the dirt and froth of newborn warriors in the gilt
of an already tarnished day themselves attack to fuse
and ground of their undone eternity spears
that slice the forbidding airs and clouds the hoarse
cries of gods who have failed and to sleep not tonight
but never in the tresses unkempt of your delirium
me to know ! a thin film unreels in the brain
a hallucination of herbs and incantations
alas and alone the leaf you set aside
the space of time before and after
the silenced mind has said its last
farewell

12-17-20

THE HIATUS

do we remember who we are
passing from room after room
always the same room with mirrors
and copies of ourselves becoming unborn
statuettes effigies of shadows nameless
asleep but awake in a light borrowed
from another time or planet and harrowing
incisions in the leaves of strange cries
prolonged in the vast antechamber
where we seem to take on appearances
tender submissions to the private Hour
allotted to our re-encounter to our falling in love
to our learning alphabets and fingertips
assuming a summer is upon us and fields
unfolding on the western slope of a page
fading from the spectrum of color and weight
recalling little of what we did the first time
an evocation of voices and grass and the sudden
sun in its intensity of blackness and echo
like a language just beyond the scope of hearing
forgetting to turn the corner where the clinic
forms the margin between past and present
this absent moment when hands apply
for a new signature and the breviary
of ashes and youth dissolves evidence
retinue of vowel and routine pronunciations
of something newly acquired the accent
and vein and of the circumflex and sighting
just above the cliffs of dew and error a bird
the many birds the wings and troth of breath
again relive the monument of separation

did you become me or are we worried
that the photograph is counterfeit the egress
into a chamber where memory is redressed
and the foils of an unspoken thought abiding
in smoke and grief a loss the total undying
we have become the chastened of spirit
the slight integers of yearning at day's end
to summon to mind the immense hiatus

12-17-20

A MEDITATION ON DEATH

who is to judge which of the *others* is the right one ?
the shape of night emerges from beneath eyelids
distorted by fever and illusion a mythology of
hypercorrections and broken temperature gauges
innocent the hand that forgets how to hold !
Atropos not *Dionysus* cuts the flower-head
with the gilded scissors of aphasia allowing
the remaining colors to dissolve in the winds
blown nightly from the Caucasus to the ruins
of the green lakes of Arcadia and who is to answer
for the repercussion in the ear without sound
a semiology of vowels without meaning a dissension
of hemispheres shifting toward an orient of skins
flayed animals altar pieces half erected scaffoldings
from which hang the shadows of the unborn and
to ask was this the child to be the golden shimmer
like pollen on the wings of butterflies the sweet
skimming surfaces of speech and to linger and sing
who is to question if fate has not already dealt its
hammer on the fragility of reason the plaything
among the wild grasses that run up-hill to nowhere
memories leave their fading imprint on legends of air
the fluted columns of the great unseen *separation*
of consciousness from rock that no messenger of the gods
can extricate from the speculation of time and
as to grief the porous formations of cliff and drill
the finality of the day's first unexpected hour holding
to the empty bosom the chasm of breath which is
nothing more than scattered atoms that cannot be
reassembled and to night return the unshaped pattern
mourning that the leaf can be no more than a passage
darkening against the glass of enigma and sleep

in a single life can one become the *other* ?

12-18-20

from the BELLUM CIVILE

joy it was the waters sprinkled victory
with spears of blood the day's enamel
smeared with lip gloss the future of the Sun
fans of air and cloudy eyes sculpted in
the brought forth head of the loser his glare
a glaze of contempt and winds that scour
without missing a dot the fissures on high
not Mercury but Minerva her foot trod
the spewed resemblances underwater of
the class a fleet of triremes and rowers
grunting a-sweat their brows furrowed
with ignorance of speech and latitude it
was a wonder to splay cloaks of porphyry
blackening as was the west a height of lists
declensions of irregularities the Egyptian
chrome peeling from the bliss of eternity
mummified like a movie actress plucking
from the sky a bird of fantastic wingspan
and to her breast clasps hitting a high-C
in her aria O virtue is Caesar clearly one
to be remembered a scattering of perukes
the legends of symbol and acrimony the fields
blossom tripartite columns of philology aching
sands longing forever the song of pyramids
bringing back the home without a door a
fossil scarab the mind ! twice or thrice
the movie unwinds its vertigo of pellucid light
other planets a score of numerals in reverse
the legible moment squandered by death

12-18-20

THE SIRENS SONG

simul aethere plena corusco
                    Valerius Flaccus

aphonic cries of a god trapped in his own myth
to speak to cliffs and border the absent skies
with plutonium and mercury the distraught
step-mother the sister cast in marble overwhelmed
speech in diptychs of rock and lichen of libel
in phonetic mistrust the symbolism and waifs
pounding at the nether gates but who can escape
the frenzied silence of the great after-thought
when death and its combination of consonants
rides the upper turf with steeds swart and glistening
stolen from steamy Aurora this song divides into
hoof and horn dew-drop and fainting leaf the once
and almighty beginning of things a rampant unseen
force drilling through the zephyrs and monuments
of ethereal distance the colonnades where glyph
and tongue encounter the fixed embolism of space
a corruption of sound and the ear in its amaze to
realize the repercussion of an archaic stream
adjacent to the narrows inhabited by the Nymphs
glories of insomnia and delusion the lapwing and
kestrel circling and diving into the foamy rage
of the last sea known to mortals and tied to mast
and singing the rope of finality Ulysses the most
of strangers the husband-to-be of Circe daughter
of the sun the malevolent twigs and spindle sigma
and conjunction of the unutterable phrase numinous
and abject the rushing grasses take knees by surprise
the kilt and down of heroes stripped and fierce
the jaw and the echo of bone himself untied from
the soul and spent a wing adrift in the eddies of air
once twice and a third time light makes its phantom
appearance in the theater of clouds where the other
god uncovers his face and brays tumultuous and wild
the lasting notes of an opprobrium of knowledge does
then all calm down the shattered harp-strings shivering
before the new-born flames of Aetna setting the Island
on its spine as the invisible and toxic choirs summon
the source of evenings to their taciturn crematorium
far below the hairline of the stars all night unbound
and stone and delta submerge into pharaonic depths
shift of hue and endless hills leaf and summer heat
nothing more can be heard but the infinite cicada

12-19-20

THE INSOMNIA OF MEDEA
for Solomon Rino

*cemetery bathed in a phosphorescent hypnosis
the blanks in between stellar points the dot
dot dot asterisks in motion the blazing sentence
on its way out the straw palace the copies
of Medea in a theogony of lost virtues each
god with his other kneeling before the golden
branch the ore-plated thoughts of desire funded
at the root by soils granular tensions the boat
itself a refrain in the second dactyl or spondee
water and its opposite a grammar of repercussions
a stone's throw and grown warriors out their
eyes in wild disdain applause on broken stone
scraped the elbows chafed the shoulders burnt
dust in motionless curtains the sky a small
resemblance to itself in the upper left quarter of sleep
would morrow ever come the tease of light
a hap and a coil the day's unfailing spiral out
of control as is the adze and the anvil against
the shot-put and the odes recited in the silent
dialect of Boeotia hemispheres of memory
the disease of mortality spelled in tiny flares
a fuse and a tin the fiction of mirrors a hand
can only wonder at its double the specter
shifting into the domain of color and gravity
peplos without hem slip-waist covert action
love at the stables brought to yoke smitten
quadrupeds and the brazen hoof the tongs
that extract thought the herbs wetted in spit
to please Juno ! rooks in phonetic formation high
on the terrible vocalism of Hecate lunations
and solar homophones the black density of Tau
as if to step and walk and breathe marble the
eye plummets inventing its own distraction
a shadow lacking definite articles the orient
come to her feet astral signatures of pyramids
at last outweighing on the scales the feather
juxtaposed to the human soul and imperfection :
leaves the size of evening and utter silence*

12-20-20

FRAGMENTS FROM THE EPOCH OF LAVA

colloquial formations of rock jutting out
against an imagined sea the lost souls of men
still attached to their oars and the baked noon
that turns mountains into pools of isolated ink
fissures and totemic planets circling in wild ellipses
just north of the moon whose fragrant appearance
at daylight's most mournful moment is a surprise
the embodiment of thought in a statue of heated marble
and infancies and childhoods symbols of grief
the quotidian mourning the symposia of madness
the market-place fills with philosophers and mountebanks
each is a fragment of the *other* ! paraphernalia
of grammar and substrata of sound yet does anything
amount to the great puzzle of solemnity and silence ?

thinking is a riddle a porous exclamation in stone
the edges of time worn down by frictions of echo and
color the brightest hue the red that intonates mantras
in the dizzy spell suffered by the physician before
he makes the first cut and whatever else eludes reason
juxtaposed to trophies of beauty and eloquence insanity
the horses hewn from basalt quarried in the pharaonic mind
still parade before the august text of endless waters
the deployment of vowels the incision of consonants
the enormous rambling of a cyclopean body tossed
into hounds-ditch *has everything gone blind ?*

iterations are never final the doxology and ideogram
of entelechy a poetry that cannot be subdivided into sand
and shore the rushing darkness that measures leaves
homophones of light the delivery of tree and epistle
what ! the fictions of air replete with noise shimmering
distances where memory lapses in the crippled grasses
that yearn for hills and so much else that was foretold
on the great islands where above all sorrow and nymphs
wash the streets with lava and phonetic decay corrodes skies
diminishing the world's imitations with a single tumult
the Pleiades have run dry and in the wastelands outside
of Siracusa a stone ear listens intently for the silence
that comes when the cosmos has run its course

12-20-20

THE UNSPEAKBLE HYMN TO HECATE
et saevo cum nox accenditur auro
Valerius Flaccus

pray to the gods no other life but this one
enough ! the world beneath the eyelids
skateboard dancer out of control the brain
kaleidoscope of derangement and reason
the mad suture that runs up the spine the loss
of nerve the ineffable contest of summer and memory
et cetera the fox racing his tail the vertigo
of windows during a sound-blast the epicure
and the synecdoche the illegal lamps and fuses
of the *deity* who governs hallucination and trance
the first of all I never said or did it and why
continue into the all-governing darkness *Hecate !*
the three-branched silence the crossed universes
the sky before the stars were born a chasm
enormous monosyllable of the uncounted rain
tragedy and its step-sister in dialogue with those
who have no accounting bedrock and stamen
the language of shadows and statues inimitable
talking to those again who have without sense
gone under wrapped in the stained white peplos
of Prosepina and the ravages of Umbrian texts
dioxide and sulfur written backwards the heights
on the small promontory ejected by Trinacria
spouting fugues of illegible fires and toxins
the cemetery where air lies buried all hush
the mums and cypresses the slender moons a-faint
in their tributaries of dearth and emptiness aloud
ancient systems of hands and grasses yearning
as ever for the fallen hills the excavated gases
Hecate ! unfathomable misery of the number two
and the children who after fifty years are still ten
and the most archaic of thoughts a drill and its stone
enter the wary into the passage of vocalic tumult
the geminated consonant at the back of the mouth
encephalitis and ring-worm bracken and algae
gorgeous floating in phosphorescent waters
to gain what ? a lifetime of elbows worn by grief
the fear of knees when the clock strikes thirteen
redundancies of distance in the perforated ear
each is the indefinite other of the unproclaimed self
a wooden Thoth sitting on a piano-note sparks
the atmospheres with a dozen relics of lightning
fossils of phonetic decay and repercussion
of the diphthongs of chalk dissolving nightly
when aching to forget the mind goes over and over
its race-track looking for the finish line *Hecate !*
and when night is ignited by its savage gold

12-21-20

THE ENCOUNTER OF THESEUS AND ARIADNE

they look at one another mistaking a goddess
for a smile a verse for the running sea that rounds
the earth in a matter of seconds the falling sky
the burning clouds the incense of unfinished dreams
is the hand to reach or mouth to yearn and gloss
and polish of the outer skin the planets wear
when the great cycles come to a close he looks
at her she wipes her lips the *next* time is nocturnal
when cliffs rush to meet the bottoms of the wave
sensational moments of silent dialogue *Amor*
abyss between sentient beings and dismissed by
words reduced to mere cavities of sound each
displays the other a fan of replicated landscapes
colors that have no meaning in the spectrum hills
lavish as waters breaking through the eyelids' scheme
and echo that is three times greater than silence
distance that sews the sun to its blackened crib
do horses then race to domains where left-branching
languages hold sway the imperfect vision of arbors
the rustle of indigo in its unborn chemistry the heavens
at last the foment of lyrics each to the other sings
all labyrinths on alert and ash and potting soil
inches of the diameter of space where fossil vowels
turn to glass and insects prey on dark consonants
do they recognize the mirror each fingers with regret
do they *know* ? or is sleep the roaring fragment
of the rock in which they steep their thoughts
a loss of breath and leaf the endless tapestry

12-21-20

STROPHES ON THE ARRIVAL OF WINTER

the reeds the rocks the rafts of thought
is this where music comes from ?
the stone-lipped angel of anesthesia who
hovers the Island now missing of Artemis
the mistaken identities the broken names
the Zeta of circumference and a thousand
lesser deities who morph into stairwells
and hiatuses and the veils of plunder
and gas the surgical nuisance of the mind
afloat on its galactic error the myriad stars
still being born in the radial symmetry
of another universe the parallels of
glass and sound the copies of antiquities
unearthed in the errant wood statues
that govern speech and the loudest vowel
of all in the funnel of understanding when
all is erased and the child within ponders
the lesson of string and wind the lightning
that comes but once and strikes in half
nascent happiness with shifts of grief
which knees must bear deep into night
what *darkness* this season spells a myth
a legend of fractured waters the ruins
of reflection and repercussion in cities
built of a single massive rock and temples
darker still with advertisements for lamps
cudgels and nails and fright-wigs to be
worn on winter solstice but for the wound
profound incision in the skull of memory
ancient straits capsized leagues and ships
and wharfs and hills of thundering mica
the shining in the distance no eye can seize
the ear taken by hives of gravity and loss
humming iridescence when sleep can be
no more and the wild natives of intensive
care whose deployed stocks of mercury glow
uncanny vestiges of haunted hexameters
consonants of smoking powder and moons
twice the size of ink that circle like syllables
in Circe's vast and oriental mouth
what is the last word a sleeping leaf can say ?

12-22-20

THE ENCOUNTER WITH EZRA POUND IN THE NEW YORK PUBLIC LIBRARY : LO MIO SERVENTE CORE

"Pliades et madidis rorantes crinibus ignes"
                                        Valerius Flaccus

have entered the palaces of black ice
refuge of the tri-syllabic sun where stunned
realia of light and distance are sundered
by repercussions of ignorance and learning
and through the marble of stairs and wells
did make way dazzled by the Orphic sound
to the throne by Circe prepared that shone
with borrowed luminescence of false gold
copies of the heavens silhouettes of lightning
bravura of economic theory and thunder
roaring through oval mementos of silence
faint reminiscence of wave descending on wave
upon shores where abandoned shields
lit signals to a glabrous indifferent sky
then saw a scarab dancing in the dense air
whose voice was that of Emperor Domitian
relic of stone resounding in the lost realms
burning tissues of unrepeated histories
the great transmogrified and unholy quest
whose was that single drop of blood that
stained the forest floor ? dazed the mask
penetrating the pantographic film of time
the hieratic beard pointing to the oceans
and to wake with someone else's soul
in one's own bed and to realize the body
has lost its space in the relentless light
these were the hours when looking high above
sea-birds circled crying with human voice
demanding back what was never given
surge of ruined waters atmospheres denied
ceaseless mourning in the pounding surf
rock and spume hands that reach for clouds
colors no one has ever seen racing the eye
to the still point of an unknown radius
homophones of planets out of tune plunging
with their hair ablaze into the *Phlegethon*
and there did stop and hush bilateral around
the dais where sat the Poet half blind with age
stoked no desires recited no hieratic verse
day's end on drum-skins of spotted deer
into what unnumbered night returned a
manicomio of *trobar clus* a cell for grief
glyphs and tombs the very leaves that
bleeding imitate fossil *Erinyes*

12-23-20

FOURTH YEAR LATIN

as far as I ever got can proceed no farther
distances are only forgeries of forgotten verbs
request for time just one more day the afternoon
when running like a painted silhouette down
sidewalks that parallel bifurcated space to
where the drug-store and its copy sit monolithic
in the spear-head light of *Diomedes* of god-like cunning
I race myself in tandem with someone else
whose resemblance is phantomatic and whose voice
is like a leaf torn in half by reason a cry
to enter realms beyond description
to libraries behind the book of staves and glyphs
going in and out of pictures colored like hills
no one has ever seen in sunsets bathed in ichor of the gods
a transom toward the other universe where Mary Lou
sits spinning Spanish gold with photographs of fingers
and the little pyramids of a poem that never ends
this is the classroom this the chalkboard of contest
to decline third declension nouns and suffer
the abacus of Roman multiplications with numerals
like graffiti of clouds and notes passed back forth
hands sweating with treachery and the dance
of Cadmus and Harmony about to blow !
will never move beyond the classroom bell
the frantic instant when everything becomes the *past*
does no one remember what we said in that rush
of tempests broken masts and tattered sail ?
vowels of wind the shape of porphyry and kisses
redolent of Pompeii pizza lipstick the end of time
scribbled in Oscan on a fallen garden wall
tiny putti with gazes of blank eternal eyes
mosaics of crossed demons and women !
the corn fields rippling with deathless summer
and there lay the corpses down one by one
until now reach close to my 82nd year
the moment of discarded memory
oblivion's text-book recitation

12-23-20

ODE : CHRISTMAS EVE 2020

when breath becomes unbearable and light
                               that offends
the thread that carries the weight the body
tripped for flight the verses of agony and strife
seen to reflect their faces otherwise and sections
of habitable air the blaze that informs the eye
                                   that swarms
with steeples of distant flares the hive and abyss
the interaction between syllable and conjunction
and if words lifted from their incoherence
were to become pure *sound* would their meaning
                                 be not greater ?
simplicity and illusion the human foil undone
the tracking backwards to the cave and incense
in rotating spirals while drumheads make signs
to the ear the end is come this frightful season
of blackened sun and riddled mountain-top
how far does the ship veer off course ?
however many the levels underneath 'til
Pluto's throne is met with grievance and flailing
who yields the scepter if not his clambering other
                                 the shadow morph
receptacle of thought the inactive and doubled glass
resonance and reduction of echo in winter's afternoon
do these kids who come sounding through the window to
break and spark their toys have evidence of life ?
to name a few the deities of stone and quicksilver
the maternal distinction of hand and file the lost
the multiples of the dead the mourning ivy on the wall
which is the direction missed the anguish of the knee
the leaf and its hidden speech tongues and blood
the legends from the grasses that darken by midday
how high the augur's guess the wings that zoom
the photographs that testify to love !
now chiaroscuro alone retains the fading shape
the bride the orange-flowers the traipsing carpet
designed to resemble tumultuous seas the breakers
the winds sent harrowing from the grotto and much else
           descent the one-way path through the wood
and mingles the archaic noun with its frailty of noise
and this day seized from the labyrinth of light
and breath the cumulation of desires to name as one
        the body and its sleeping otherness the loss
incomplete heavens fractioned half of time
the guiding star alone the abstract vowel amiss
the smoke-house and gather ashes all

12-24-20

SONNET : DIANA IN WINTER

that means all we ever saw was the underneath
the fluted drain the shallows where no feet shod
the linger apse the collateral frail sending its shift
aloft the roof and tentacle of desire the many of
the loss a delicacy to respire if evenings long shot
the gone and other the finger lingering in the song
of grass ear-foil and stain of sound the event night
hauls across the burdened hills steep as moaning
pack animals the brief to retort a god so loud a
thunder and basilisk in the cyclical sand and white
heat reddening shafts Diana in her ire no hunt starts
across the slight domain the width of time an ink
that sprawls its signature of pyramids and aching
breast to her hold dear the winter noise of silence

12-24-20

TWO STANZAS XMAS 2020

we have gone through the seven repertoires
flipped the pages of the incongruent encyclopedia
worshipped at the altar of solar homophones
in the blackening dusk of world-end the fumous
and inglorious disregard for prior births the candle
and lighting ceremony of the child who cannot be
the lessons of whiplash and undertow the loud
and salmon-colored twilight a distance of forty ells
twice have recognized and just as fast forgotten
the face wedged in between three mirrors and
listening without success for the red-stained tone
how echo was the difference how void its naked stone
the content of the cloud suppressed its abashed tongue
a statue of pure air shadows of incorporeal weights
the wood and rock of the unending hour the lice
that swarm the dark consonants of the moon
how much is never clear and how slight the bone
inserted between human vowels and their abyss
the cave of activity and metaphor the recitations
spoken like frank-incense in the martyrs' lodge
too soon we'll know too hard we'll reel the song
from Hindustan revealed its aching throb of sound
its melody of rivers running dry the heights of love
desire's unemployed syllables and latest least of
never the earth longing for its leafy mysteries

the second half of life which is really the greater
yet more minimal the rocky slope otherwards to
hemispheres outside the light no chance to regret
the Himalayan draught focus on palpitating hearts

does sleep halve the upper hand the bipartite column
the missing voice the leaf and lattice of memory
off the beaten path stray woods and the curule seat
to lessen the sun's already lost homophone thought
in its circular divestment of territory aching to
have none of it back each prelude to darkness
the dosage of night where mingle the persons
whose names no longer match the faces worn
like silver masks that used to adorn the living room
when the gong would sound erasing vowels from
the system of mind that claims to own music
since it is chaos that brings order to the copied note
ascension of the Lord in a puff of deranged napalm
is to chorus the repetitions of opium in perfume
the faint strain of orient in the strewn boudoir
1978 in the Hotel Durant and the already phased
moon in its sandalwood shell shining divinity
of jazz carved into the furious cloud-work of ideas
that perpetrate the grave error of mortality a
scale of ringing and the fast ear that holds nothing
the living wax the buzz of the meridian insects sawing
through the teeth of corn in the deathless summer
of stuttering heat and adolescence the broken branch
and at last hills doomed in ocher and defiance
when windows have no more domain nor skies

12-25-20

COMPASSION FOR THE LIVING
COMPASSION FOR THE DYING

for Rob Elder

thoughtlessness brings confusion and sorrow
smoke from the burning rock in the midst of the sea
ascending turned the once shining ether black
nor did the heroes over-wrought with home-sickness
know which way to compass their skiff
the deaths of the many weighing heavy in the night
bracketed illusions and the larger parenthesis of breath
the stiffest reprimands from the hidden vault of sky
the very voice pounding from the anvil reverberating
from cloud to cloud and the fear that comes before sleep
the nocturnal hive and flurry of unseen wings
what was to expect ? the shores and lands in mists
were but a fading memory pallid vestige of life
among trees and grasses the meadows of childhood
fleeting vision of maids tossing a spherical object
on the sandy mounds hard-by the foaming waves
would one never play this again the round of branches
turning silver by mid-afternoon and the roulette
of the gods making all seem as laughter and sport
'til the dawn that wreaks the unwanted day breaks
and one by one puzzled mortals stagger
this way and that looking for the key to harmony
a waste of bone and soot the distances of fields
untilled and full of stifling heat the unimaginable
how is the shoulder to bear this gravity ?
look to the thin western route the waters that come
pouring through the sluice giving birth to the stars
the uncountable assembly of thoughts the heights
loud with an unforgivable silence to have known
and not understood ! waking beside an absence
a shadow of mind and to go on through the wood
the haunted leaves of voices betrayed by ignorance
and the bleeding trellis and the flayed skins
of innocent spotted deer that strayed from the paddock
into what maze had the heroes fallen ?
to learn anew the mysteries cannot be apprehended
the small reef where come to rest the survivors
and not tell a soul what is to be done to what fastness
hold the frail vowel promised of infinity
the dripping hour the unending waters
a hand that once owned shape
a finger weeping to the bone
which is the *one* and who is the *other* ?

12-25-20

CIRCE'S TOYS

terrific noise coming from nowhere
have we woken up against the will of Zeus ?
who bids us to empty handed go to the altar
first fruits entrails hapless deer hides a drum
of unreason to send smoking into the dewy airs
the fragrances dear to the pointless deities
who run the show a few miles above the surface
and don we pelts and stumble chanting nonsense
to an invisible bride resuscitated from some adolescent
prayer-wheel and recall of how she went under ?
for what is the step to take and which is the way
to enter the wood come the propitious hour
blind hacks strumming broken lutes the pyre
of imagination the blaze that requires no thunder
how is the shore come to us so quickly ?
dappled knees waters of ruined mirages a city !
as quick as are the silences of light and opprobrium
led us into the lair she did and set us against each other
sharpening the music against files of redundancies
saying this is literature these are the oracle bones
this is the text written in the soil these the furrows
where heat spells the future of each illegible
and stood we then stunned before the unfinished cairn
stone heap and deliquescent shapes indefinable
as the language that bore them and staring to turn
watching the air consume itself and fiery globes
from a distance the zooming metaphysics
all sound and no meaning the manifest particles
the cyclotron would smash beneath the bleachers
summon forth your dead ! boomed the voice of entelechy
bid us devour blackened leaves and a retort
of infamous legends the hill slopes of ocher din
massive echoing ballistics of some Olympian challenge
stood then the mountain newly risen before
and the myriad paths scuttled shields gleam
of dragon eyes the specific and the undefined together
with teeth ! the miasma of Agamemnon and the phantom
of Cassandra sporting like a weird sprite on the steps
a cigarette in each hand and the loosened hair pins
and dazzle of bare shoulders a vision and gone
nothing but the whisper of grasses underfoot
syllables of glass the voice of Demeter half a foot
from the inch that surrounds the unfinished moment
how to proceed which vowel to place before the other
lunacy and craven desires the earthly lot
against the will of Zeus ! the sigma of the orient
the lessons of baleful phonetic decay asbestos and
rinds and husks detritus of human thought
it was never to go back again to the House
it was nostalgia and longing for the seas of morning
for the rope and skein for the laboring hand
that weaves love into the portion of deeds
and us ? o'erwhelmed beasts Circe's toys
junket and spruce jazz and reversed calendar
our day our never-ending day !   12-26-20

ALAS ! THOU DOST LEAVE OUR WOODLAND

                                      the fix between music
and its counterpart *nonsense* the sounds that
dissolve meaning and the sense of air as activity
the famous longing for ether and accumulation
of depths the poor Latin inconstancy of vowels
judged not for their shape but for their weight
a lasting loss of innocence the bricklayer's dream
of intransigence the heights Madame Blavatsky
considered as pure number—are you with me ?
the spiral staircase with its lit cigarettes as
well as the suspended brain the excavation
of thought the dry-run to the oriental pronoun
in search of the rivers that run underground
bearing with them language and its pre-history
phonetic attacks on the body the grassy spears
that maim the toxic norm the wasted folds
misery the human pox ascension of literature
as a single deranged monosyllable shattered
at the touch of glass and heat the formations
of aerial glyphs and swooping wings of light
flux of bee and analphabetic digits clouds inks
everything that can be written on a grain of sand
the pharaonic utterance that stupefies the ear
sleeping in its hive of frozen consonants steep
in the daft moment when day turns to reverie
memory of the instantaneous mirror of re-death
is the mind blind from birth ? discontinuous breath
sketches of an out-of-body repercussion painted
green the oath of animus to anima and swooning
hummingbird and serpent skill-set of the twins
doubled refractions of water lifted by lever
to the seventh repertoire and the paean and fill
of the skies crescendo of atavism and disorder
when the sacred collides with aphasia wearing
funereal white the disrobing of Radha the familiar
versus the chthonic
                                      aggravation and perpetuity

of the wheel ! come no closer *Rudra* !

at this point the Muses fail me
affinity to breath !   copies of air !
in what unwritten epic do I wake undiscovered ?
the Nymphs are born again
                                      the rooftops sprout leaves !

12-27-20

finis

TAMAZUNCHALE

Berkeley CA
6-20-20/12-27-20

Poetry by Iván Argüelles

Published by

Luna Bisonte Prods:

DIARIO DI UN OTTOGENARIO [2020]

TWILIGHT CANTOS [2019]

CIEN SONETOS [2018]

LAGARTO DE MI CORAZÓN [2018]

FRAGMENTS FROM A GONE WORLD [2017]

LA INTERRUPCIÓN CONVERSACIONAL [2016]

ORPHIC CANTOS [2015]

D U O P O E M A T A :
ILION—A TRANSCRIPTION
& ALTERTUMSWISSENSCHAFT [2015]

FIAT LUX [2014]

A DAY IN THE SUN [2012]

ULTERIOR VISIONS [2011]

All are available at:

https://www.lulu.com/spotlight/lunabisonteprods

or www.spdbooks.org

www.ingramcontent.com/pod-product-compliance
Lightning Source LLC
Chambersburg PA
CBHW071202160426
43196CB00011B/2173